THE CALL OF A CAREGIVER

finding comfort, pursuing purpose

2 Corinthians 4:17

the
CALL OF A
CAREGIVER
a true story

finding comfort, pursuing purpose

Jessica Mast

AMBASSADOR INTERNATIONAL
GREENVILLE, SOUTH CAROLINA & BELFAST, NORTHERN IRELAND

www.ambassador-international.com

The Call of a Caregiver
finding comfort, pursuing purpose

Printed in the United States of America

ISBN: 9781935507642

Cover & Layout Design by David Siglin
Photography of hands by Justin and Holly Smith
Flourish illustration courtesy of: *www.designious.com*

AMBASSADOR INTERNATIONAL
Emerald House
427 Wade Hampton Blvd.
Greenville, SC 29609, USA
www.ambassador-international.com

AMBASSADOR BOOKS
The Mount
2 Woodstock Link
Belfast, BT6 8DD, Northern Ireland, UK
www.ambassador-international.com

The colophon is a trademark of Ambassador

Dedication

I DEDICATE THIS BOOK TO my beloved late husband, Jimmy, who endured and ultimately triumphed over so much. May others read of your courage, strength, and faith in the Lord while displaying a loving gentleness that will never be forgotten. Till we meet again . . .

I also dedicate this book to my Uncle David Amick, my mother's brother, who went to heaven at the young age of 20. Let this book honor your life and your own love of writing, an inspiration to me. I look forward to meeting you on the day our Lord calls me home.

Nathan James Wall, Jr. "Jimmy"
June 17, 1978 –
June 17, 2006

David Ray Amick
August 19, 1950 –
January 29, 1971

Foreword

HOW DO YOU HANDLE AN unexpected and sudden change in your life? My daughter, Jessica, not only faced it but walked through it with humility, strength, and courage by the grace given her from our Lord and Savior, Jesus Christ. Jessica and her husband, Jimmy, had plans, hopes, and dreams for their future as all young couples do, looking forward to an abundant life. With the sudden onset of his illness, their faith was challenged.

During the months of Jimmy's illness, he showed patience, never complaining, but looked to God, the Author and Finisher of our faith. Jessica cared for him with such beauty and grace as only she could by the strength given her from above.

As you read her story, you will feel as though you are walking by her side on this amazing journey of faith. You will experience the ups and downs, the hopes and expectations she and Jimmy felt. And, ultimately, how she experienced the disappointment of Jimmy's early passing.

But in all of this, through perseverance and endurance, faith is again found and we see how God always leads us in triumph (2 Corinthians 2:14). Jimmy's faith brought him to his heavenly home; Jessica's courage in suffering brought her to rest and trust in the steadfast love of God.

— JANET BRANNON, *Jessica's mom*

Acknowledgments

IT AMAZES ME HOW GOD provides all that you need to accomplish what He's called you to do. I'm most grateful for the wonderful people whom God called to come into my life and walk along beside me on this journey to complete this book—God's work.

I first and foremost thank my wonderful husband, PJ. Thank you for your belief in me to write a book about the most painful time in my life so that others can see the heart of God. Your support, prayers, and wisdom brought me through the process. You truly sacrificed for this book to be completed, and for that, I can't thank you enough.

Thank you to Elizabeth Morrisey, writer, photographer, author of *Firm Foundations: A Tour of Upstate Presbyterian Churches* and co-author of *God's Lineup.* Not only did you help with my editing process, but your encouragement helped in so many ways. Thank you for contacting Ambassador International for me . . . more evidence of how God works in awesome ways!

I must thank Beth Marshall, author of *A Time to Heal, a grief journal.* Your mentorship has provided much wisdom and spiritual guidance for me. Thank you so much for always being available to answer my many questions.

Thank you, Tim Lowry at Ambassador International, for giving me this opportunity to publish my story. Thank you for all of your guidance through the writing and publishing process and for helping me to become established as an author.

Thank you to my brother, Justin Smith, and sister-in-law, Holly Smith, for your contribution to the cover design and for your prayers. Justin, you are such a talented graphic designer, and I'm so proud of you. Thank you for your encouragement in the Lord when I needed it and for being an awesome brother.

I don't know what I would have done without the help of my mom, Janet Brannon, and stepdad, Mike Brannon. Mom, your spiritual encouragement, motherly wisdom, and friendship provided me with strength when I needed it. All the time that you gave to take care of our little Catherine enabled me to finish the book in God's timing. Mike, thank you for taking the time to review medical information with me during both Jimmy's illness and my writing process. Thank you both so much for always being there for me.

Thank you to my dad, John Smith, and stepmom, Sandy Smith, for all of your support and encouragement. Thank you for being there for me and always being available when I needed your suggestions. God's provided me with such amazing parents.

To the parents who have remained very dear to my heart, James and Geneva Wall, I appreciate your continuous love and support for me. Not only were you such wonderful and loving parents to Jimmy, but you took me in as your daughter as well. That means more to me than I can say.

Thank you to Jimmy's sister, Kathy Cox, and her husband, Kenny Cox. Thank you for caring about me like a sister and for all of your help and support for me to write this book.

Thank you to my sister, Jennifer Broome, my brother-in-law, Chris Broome, my nephews, Camron Bannister and Landon Broome, my Aunt Betsy Love, and my wonderful grandparents, Seber and Mildred Amick, for your encouragement and prayers for me while writing the book. I needed that so much.

To PJ's mom, Catherine Mast, his dad, Paul Mast, and sisters, Cathy Kramer, Rose Cooley, and Iris Lyndaker and their families, thank you above all for opening your hearts to me and where I came from. To have your care and support has blessed me in many ways. I love you all and am so thankful for you.

Thank you to the following physicians and medical staff who cared for Jimmy, not only with your medical expertise but with your hearts as well:

Dr. Leonard Pugh, Internal Medicine, Greenville, SC; the doctors at Gastroenterology Associates, Greenville, SC; Dr. W. Larry Gluck, Hematology/Oncology, Greenville, SC.

At the Medical University of South Carolina (MUSC): Dr. Ira Willner and Dr. Adrian Reuben. Also, thank you to the nursing staff who cared for Jimmy.

At Duke University Hospital: Dr. Murat Arcasoy, Dr. Joseph Moore, Dr. Jon Gockerman, Dr. Louis Diehl, and all the physicians at Duke who contributed to Jimmy's care. Also, thank you to the phenomenal oncology nurses; to Kristy Everette, Oncology Recreation Therapist; and to Michael Paul Brown, Patient Resource Manager. You cared deeply for both Jimmy and me when we needed it the most.

I want to thank the following individuals whom Jimmy and I worked with at Guardian Building Products: Duane Faulkner, Wayne Scott, Martin Powell, David Love, and all coworkers to Jimmy and me. Thank you for going beyond the responsibilities of an employer and for being there for us like a family.

Thank you to Apostles Ron and Hope Carpenter and Elders Rick and Judy Smith at Redemption World Outreach Center in Greenville, SC, for your spiritual leadership to Jimmy and me. Thank you, Elders Rick and Judy, for taking me under your wing and being there for me during my most difficult times of grief. Also, thank you to Patrick and Danielle Figueroa for your spiritual mentorship and close friendship to Jimmy and me. Thank you for all you did for us in our most difficult times.

To Pastor Perry Noble at NewSpring Church in Anderson, SC, thank you for your spiritual leadership to PJ and me and for your bold teaching that pushes us to do all that God has called us to do.

Thank you to Jimmy, by beloved late husband, the one who endured so much and who I believe may have laid down his life for the gospel of Jesus Christ to reach even further. This is your story and your testimony for the glory of God. Thank you for your love for me and for all that you gave.

Above all, I thank my Lord and Savior, Jesus Christ. He paid the ultimate price for Jimmy to now have perfect peace and healing in his heavenly home. And because of His sacrifice, our separation is only temporary. Jesus, I praise You.

Table of Contents

Jimmy and Jessica's Wedding Picture
September 6, 2003

From left to right: Kathy Cox (Jimmy's sister), Jimmy,
and Geneva and James Wall (Jimmy's parents)

CHAPTER I

Our Beginning
My Hopes and Dreams
(AUGUST 2002–DECEMBER 2005)

I LOOKED ACROSS THE CHURCH sanctuary, and there he was, sitting quietly with his Bible in his lap waiting for the service to start. On this warm Wednesday evening in August of 2002, I subtly looked his way in attempt to make eye contact with him and catch his attention. A month earlier was when I had seen him for the first time. My, he was good looking! Questions had been running through my mind . . . *Is he single? How old is he? Is his heart right with God? What does he do for a living?* I really wanted to meet him.

I had just graduated from college and was excited and looking forward to my future, knowing there were so many wonderful possibilities. After dedicating my life to Jesus earlier that spring, I was full of anticipation of what God had for me next. I knew the desires of my heart: to be a wife to a strong Christian husband, to have children, and to have a ministry. I wanted to live as a witness for the Lord and believed that God had all of these wonderful things for me in my future. I knew that the Bible says that we will have trials (1 Peter 4:12) and that our faith will be tested (James 1:3), but I didn't quite understand the reality of what that really meant. I was a twenty-one year old who had just finished earn-

Jimmy on a hiking trip

ing her business degree, had just dedicated her life to God, was as single as you can be, and had just started attending this awesome church in Greenville, South Carolina. Everything was all set up for God to bring amazing things into my life, and I was more than ready! So I thought. . . .

I had prayed about that tall, handsome man with dark hair who I had been eyeing for a month by then. I knew if it were the Lord's will, then our meeting would happen. *There's not a better place to meet a husband than at church*, I thought to myself. *This guy just might be "the one."*

As I exited the sanctuary after that August Wednesday night service, I knew he was walking behind me, and I felt butterflies in my stomach. As I walked into the lobby of the church, I heard this voice behind me say, "That was a great service, wasn't it?" I turned around and saw his handsome face looking down at me. I responded, trying not to sound nervous. His name was Jimmy, and he was twenty-four years old. He was in the mortgage business and had just recently moved to Greenville. By the end of the conversation, he asked me if I wanted to grab a bite to eat.

I was absolutely smitten. After some time dating and a lot of praying, we knew that God's will was for us to be married.

He was a strong Christian man with godly values, and God had blessed him with much wisdom. We dated for four months, were engaged for nine months, and married on September 6, 2003. I felt like I was the most blessed woman in the world to be the bride of this wonderful, amazing man.

While we were dating, I learned that Jimmy had diabetes and was diagnosed with it when he was just six years old. I have always had a strong nurturing instinct, and I immediately wanted to learn about what he needed and how I could help him. He had to check his blood sugar and give himself several shots of insulin every day. My mom, who is a nurse, taught me how to administer his shots, and Jimmy showed me how to check his blood sugar. He was totally able to take care of this by himself, but I wanted to know how to take care of him in case he ever needed help. This was a condition that he dealt with daily, but I was more than happy that I could be there for him. I found it joyful to do the things that I, as his wife, wanted to help with: make sure he had the medical supplies he needed, help him record his medical numbers in his notebook, and see that he got to the doctor when it was time for a checkup.

I enjoyed being there for him, loving him, and doing my best to be the wife that God called

Jimmy and Jessica
Christmas Day 2004

me to be. I by all means fell short at times; I was young and had a lot to learn. I loved Jimmy with all my heart and wanted to be there for him always. I was proud of the man that I married. He was intelligent and extremely talented in many ways, and he loved playing sports and almost all the time won at what he did. He was smart with our finances and seemed to always have the right answers to things. We did have our ups and downs with adjusting to marriage, but God was with us through it all.

We were married for two years when Jimmy began feeling badly and more tired than normal. In November of 2005, he went in for a doctor's appointment, and they found that the health of his liver was not good. The doctor seemed to think that this was possibly caused by his having the Epstein-Barr virus, a virus that is common but can cause infectious mononucleosis, also known as mono.[1] By the beginning of December, he was admitted to the hospital. We figured that after a short stay in the hospital he would recover and be okay. We believed God was allowing us to go through a small trial and that everything would be all right. Little did we know the road that God had set ahead of us, what we were about to walk through, how our faith would be tested to the extreme, and just how good our God is in the midst of severe pain, uncertainty, fear, and suffering.

This is our story. I hope for this to be a testimony of how with the power, strength, and presence of God, you can survive what looks like the unsurvivable.

---

1. *Wikipedia, the Free Encyclopedia,* "Epstein-Barr Virus," http://en.wikipedia.org/wiki/Epstein-Barr_virus (accessed February 16, 2011).

CHAPTER 2

On Our Way to the Hospital

The First Time

(DECEMBER 2005)

EARLY IN THE MORNING ON Thursday, December 8, 2005, Jimmy and I were up and getting ready for the day. I was dressing for work, and Jimmy was waking up to get ready for his appointment. His doctor had discovered a couple of weeks before that the lab results for his liver were abnormal, and he was beginning to have a pain near his stomach. They decided to make an appointment to do an ultrasound of his liver.

At the time, I was working as an Administrative Assistant for two Vice Presidents at Guardian Building Products, a company whose corporate office is in the Greenville area. Jimmy worked there as well as the manager of a division of the accounting department, which proved to be set up by God in preparation for what lay ahead of us. At that time, I had worked there a little over a year and a half, and Jimmy had worked there for a year.

I was about thirty minutes from leaving for work when I heard Jimmy call my name. I went to check on him and found that he was in the bathroom vomiting. His skin was yellow to the point that he looked like he had been painted with a yellow highlighter, and I immediately knew that he could not go by himself.

I called into work to let them know that I couldn't make it into the office, and then I helped Jimmy finish getting ready. He was still sick and feeling terrible. I didn't know what was going on but was hoping we would find out more at his ultrasound appointment.

When we arrived to the medical center, Jimmy felt too sick to even get out of the car, and he couldn't bear the thought of sitting in the waiting room full of people. I had him stay in the car while I went to sign him in for his appointment, and when they were ready for him to come back, I went to the car and helped him into the area where he was to have the ultrasound. Jimmy started vomiting again, and I was extremely concerned about his blood sugar level because of his diabetes. I was able to help him manage his diabetes on a normal day-to-day basis, but his being so sick took the medical care above what I was able to do for him. I was nervous and scared and at the same time upset to see him feeling so badly.

The ultrasound tech couldn't tell us any definite results; that was for the doctors to say. Because of the vomiting and the jaundice (yellowing of the skin), she recommended that we get in to see his doctor right away. I immediately called and insisted that he be seen by his doctor as soon as possible. The receptionist on the other end told me to bring him straight there.

We were sitting in the exam room at the doctor's office about thirty minutes later. I wanted terribly to help Jimmy feel better, but that was beyond my control. All I could do was comfort him, help him with what he needed, and be there by his side. I knew that the Lord had His hand on us, and I trusted in Him to take care of Jimmy.

His doctor, Dr. Leonard Pugh, came in to examine him. His liver was apparently not functioning properly, and they didn't know exactly why. They had several ideas but no definite answers. After considering the fact that this would make managing his diabetes more difficult, Dr. Pugh made the decision to admit him to the hospital. I felt relieved that he would be there in case things started getting worse. I didn't want to run the risk of being with him by myself at home and not knowing what to do.

After getting the paperwork and the instructions telling us where to go once we arrived at the hospital, we were on our way. I wanted to get Jimmy settled and comfortable as soon as I could. As we pulled into the parking lot, I knew I needed to call our families to let them know what was happening.

Jimmy's family lives in the small town of Hemingway, South Carolina, where he was raised. Hemingway is about a four-hour drive from Greenville toward the South Carolina coast. His parents, James and Geneva Wall (I call them Mr. James and Mrs. Geneva or Mom and Dad), are such sweet and loving people. Jimmy's older sister, Kathy, also lives in Hemingway with her husband, Kenny, and their two boys, Jacob and Jared. Jimmy truly valued family and enjoyed their close relationship.

I was extremely blessed to be married into such a warm and loving family.

I wanted to make sure that I explained what was happening to them in a way that would keep them calm. They knew he hadn't been feeling well, but I didn't want to worry them. However, they had to know that Jimmy was being admitted to the hospital. His mother, a strong woman of faith, had such a calm and peaceful voice on the other end. I explained to her everything that happened that day, and she too was thankful that the doctors would be monitoring him more closely until he recovered. I was glad to hear Mrs. Geneva's voice sounding so calm. She assured me that they would be praying for us, and I told her I would give her updates as frequently as I could.

The doctors did not indicate that this was an extreme situation. They speculated that his worsening liver functions could be due to his having mono caused by the Epstein-Barr virus. They were not concerned over this being a major ordeal because the liver is an organ that is able to repair itself. The doctors thought that after this virus ran its course, Jimmy's liver would recover and be right back to normal again.

I prayed for our situation and thanked God for the medical care that He was providing for us. After all, I figured after a few days, we would be back in the comfort of our home.

It was a cool day outside. I reached for my coat and purse, feeling a slight breeze as I opened the car door. Jimmy decided to stay in the car while I filled out the registration papers for the hospital. It wouldn't take very long, and he was more comfortable there. When I finished the registration process and was given his room number, I went out to the car to help him into the hospital. We walked through the lobby to the elevators. We got up to his room, and the nurse instructed him to put on the hospital gown. After I folded his clothes and helped him into the hospital bed, I called my mom to let her know we were in the room. We were there for Jimmy to get better. I took a deep breath and prayed.

Jimmy on his motorcycle

CHAPTER 3

From Optimism to the Unexpected

(DECEMBER 2005)

I WOKE SUDDENLY WITH A jolt as a bright light filled the room. It almost hurt as I squinted my eyes to look at the clock. The time was just past 4:00 a.m. on Saturday morning. This was about the same time the nurse had come into the room the morning before and abruptly turned on the overhead lights to draw Jimmy's blood for his daily lab tests. We had stayed in the hospital for two nights already, and he was starting to feel a little better. His vomiting had stopped, and he was able to eat something other than clear liquids.

I started going through my bag to find what I needed to get as freshened up as you can while staying in a hospital. The day that Jimmy was admitted, my mom, who lives about ten minutes away from our house, brought us some of the personal items that we needed from home. I am tremendously grateful for the wonderful mother that God gave me. She is an amazing woman of God, and we have enjoyed an especially close mother-daughter relationship. She and my stepfather, Mike, were there to help us in so many ways. The fact that they lived so close to us was a huge help, and having them there for us was an immeasurable comfort.

Jimmy handled everything incredibly well. He showed a sound strength that could be provided only by our Everlasting Father. I knew that God was with us, even in the middle of our not having any clear answers yet as to why his liver was sick. Jimmy was more of a quiet person and didn't talk much about what he was feeling. He had a high pain tolerance. If he was in pain, he showed it as little as possible. I so badly wanted us to talk more about what was going on, but I also wanted to respect his wishes if he didn't feel like having much conversation. In 2 Corinthians 12:9, Jesus said, "My grace is sufficient for you, for My strength is made perfect in weakness." We were living that scripture, and before long found how much we would be standing on that Word in the weeks and months ahead.

While Jimmy was taking his shower later that morning, I was sitting in a chair in the room when I heard a knock on the door. When I opened the door, I saw the doctor standing there. This was the gastroenterologist that was on call for the weekend. He introduced himself to me, and I let him know that Jimmy was in the shower. He told me that he could come back later to see Jimmy but that he was able to give me some information. Apparently the blood test from that morning showed that his liver had not made any improvements. The bilirubin measurement can be used to determine whether or not a person's liver is functioning properly. A normal measurement is around one, and Jimmy's was over six that day. They still couldn't confirm exactly what was causing this to happen. With all of this being taken into consideration, the doctor told me that if Jimmy didn't soon improve, they would have to transfer him to the Medical University of South Carolina (MUSC) in Charleston. If things got worse, he would need to be in a place where they could perform a liver transplant. This was a total shock to me. I never thought that we would be looking at anything as serious as that.

When Jimmy got out of the shower, I told him what the doctor had said. Even though this seemed like a shock, we just *knew* that no matter how bad things looked, our God was going to deliver us out of this at any moment. We were nervous, but we didn't really feel fearful. I just believed that the worse God allowed our situation to become, the more glory He would receive when He "rescued" us out of it. I mean, the God that we serve would surely heal Jimmy before things got too bad. Jimmy's healing would be a strong testimony for the Lord. We were just going to take the steps that God had for us to take, and we would give God all the glory *when* He made Jimmy well. I learned later on not to assume that you know what God will or will not allow to happen in your life. He knows what He needs to bring you through for His ultimate plan and for your good a lot better than you do, even if it hurts. His plans and His purposes are greater than what we have planned and purposed in our minds. And for whatever you need along the way, His "grace is sufficient"!

I had spent several days reading my Bible and doing word searches as I sat by Jimmy's bed ready at any moment to get him something that he needed. However, he was very independent and wanted to do as much for himself as possible. He remained quiet as he processed in his mind all that was happening, and I knew that he would talk more when he was ready.

Jimmy stayed stable through the weekend, and we decided that I should go back to work on Monday. Boy, was it hard to leave Jimmy to go home Sunday night. I never wanted to leave his side even though I knew the nurses would take good care of him. He was my Jimmy, and I wanted to be right there beside him to make sure he had everything he needed. He assured me that he would be just fine; I would be only a phone call and a fifteen-minute drive away.

I got home that night and tried to keep my thoughts positive as I prayed continually. Jimmy had been going through a period of time when he wasn't walking as close to the Lord as he once was. I thought maybe this was God's way of drawing Jimmy back close to Him again. I was putting my faith and trust in Jesus. He knew what He was doing with our situation. Isaiah 55:8–9 says, "'For My thoughts are not your thoughts, nor are your ways My ways,' says the Lord. 'For as the heavens are higher than the earth, so are My ways higher than your ways, and My thoughts than your thoughts.'" Even if I tried to figure out all the answers, I couldn't possibly fully understand the magnificent purposes of the Lord. That is why these things require faith. We can't understand it on our own, but our Heavenly Father Who loves us "preserves the way of His saints" (Proverbs 2:8).

Monday morning couldn't come soon enough. I called Jimmy to check on him as soon as I woke up, and he assured me that he would call when he talked to the doctor. Not long after I arrived at work, he called and told me that they were discharging him from the hospital. I was pleasantly surprised and at the same time a little unsure if he was ready to be discharged, but his lab tests revealed that he was stable and well enough to be taken care of at home. I rushed from the office to the hospital, and when I arrived, Jimmy was dressed, packed up, and ready to go.

We were glad to get into the comfort of our own home. I had a few questions that I didn't have a chance to ask at the hospital. I called his doctor to get the answers that I needed while my mother went to the pharmacy to pick up his prescriptions. We now needed to do a lot of monitoring: checking his blood sugar more frequently, checking his weight each day to make sure he wasn't retaining fluid, and checking his temperature to make sure he wasn't getting an infection. Jimmy was such a trooper through all of this, cooperating with the doctors and with me as much as he could stand. I was very busy and always wishing I could do more to make him better.

There is a certain type of burden that a caregiver carries. I could feel the Lord carrying it for me, and I had to completely rely on Him to be the source of my strength. I had to bring my own needs and feelings to Jesus so that I could be strong enough spiritually, emotionally, and physically for Jimmy. The Lord provided me with what I needed. Man alone could not help me. I looked to God to pour into me so that I could turn and pour into Jimmy. God knows what you need when you need it, and He is always faithful. The Bible says that He will never leave you nor forsake you (Deuteronomy 31:6) and that He supplies all our needs (Philippians 4:19). That is the truth!

A few days after we came home, Greenville was hit with one of the worst ice storms that I have seen in the area. Freezing rain brought down trees and power lines, leaving many people without power for almost a week. We were one of them, but thankfully our power was out for only thirty-six hours. But that was still long enough to need to pack up items from the freezer and refrigerator (including Jimmy's insulin) and our suitcases and head to my mom and stepdad's house for a night. We had no heat or hot water and had to leave. Jimmy did all he could to help me load things into the car, but I had to make sure that he didn't push himself too hard. We drove around trees in the road and patches of ice before we made it to their house.

We were grateful that our power was restored the following day, and we were back home once again. However, a few days later (just seven days after being discharged from the hospital), Jimmy started having severe pain in his abdomen. I called his doctor's office, and they advised that since the pain was that severe to go to the emergency room. They would have the doctor on call meet us there. While we were waiting in the room for the doctor to arrive, I began making phone calls to our families to let them know that we were back at the hospital. After the doctor examined him, he told us that fluid had collected in Jimmy's abdomen and that it may have become infected. They admitted him that day and scheduled to remove and test the fluid the next morning. Jimmy assured me that he was okay and that it would probably help me to get a good night's rest at home. I didn't really want to go home that night, but Jimmy convinced me. I told him I would be back very early the next morning.

I arrived back at the hospital about 6:00 a.m. to find that Jimmy had been throwing up all night. He had an allergic reaction to the pain medicine they gave him, and it caused him to be extremely ill throughout the night. After he began to feel a little better that morning, I went with him to the area of the hospital where he was to have the fluid removed from his abdomen. This was a minor procedure, and we were back in his room within a couple of hours. Jimmy continued to be a little sick from the reaction to the pain medicine. Therefore, I knew I needed to stay at the hospital with him instead of going to work.

The next day, my dad called to tell me he was planning to visit us. He lives in Columbia, South Carolina, which is about an hour-and-a-half drive from Greenville. I found it very comforting to talk to my dad; he cared for us tremendously and wanted to be there for us. Unfortunately, Jimmy was feeling too badly for company, and with the health of his liver in jeopardy, it was wise to have as few visitors as possible. My dad decided to drive up that evening to take me to dinner instead, and that meant a lot to me. After dinner that evening, Jimmy and I enjoyed the fragrance of a beautiful Christmas flower bouquet that my sister, Jennifer, and her boyfriend (now her husband), Chris, sent to us. When I saw the sweet look of comfort on Jimmy's face when he received the flowers, I felt exceptionally grateful for the loving family that we have.

The following morning, on December 22, I could tell that the allergic reaction to the pain medicine had taken a toll on Jimmy. He appeared more jaundiced, and he continued to feel poorly. The doctors discovered that the fluid around his abdomen was in fact infected, and they started him on antibiotics. I was constantly on the phone with family and friends to give them updates. The doctor told us that he had been on the phone with the hepatologist (a gastroenterologist that sub-specializes in diseases of the liver) at MUSC in Charleston to decide if Jimmy should be transferred. We knew that this was a possibility and we tried to prepare ourselves. We just wanted him to get better, and we wanted to be wherever we needed to for that to happen. Jimmy showed a tremendous amount of courage and strength through all of this. He didn't complain. He had already dealt with so much because of his diabetes, and it hurt me to see him go through this too. However, we didn't know how God was working through our situation. We had to trust in the Lord. This was not in our hands.

A little past lunchtime, the doctor came rushing into the room. Jimmy's bilirubin had spiked to over eleven, and his liver could be beginning to fail. The doctor told us the ambulance would be arriving shortly. We were headed to Charleston.

CHAPTER 4

God's Sustaining Power in New Territory
(December 2005)

As I stood in the doorway of the hospital room watching the paramedics strap Jimmy onto the stretcher, a sinking feeling settled into my heart. I had been able to be by Jimmy's side to nurture and comfort him, and now all I could do was helplessly watch as the paramedics rolled him away. Charleston is about a three-and-a-half-hour drive from Greenville, and I had to get moving in order to arrive as soon as possible behind the ambulance. After the nurses gave me the instructions on where to go once I arrived at MUSC, I rushed to get to my car. I felt the adrenaline running through me as I tried to comprehend what to expect.

My mother told me that she would not let me go alone. My stepdad printed directions for the two of us, and my mom met me with them at my house. The plan was for me to leave as soon as I finished packing bags for Jimmy and me, and she would leave soon after. We had no idea how long we would be in Charleston. As I was gathering my things, I received numerous phone calls from our church and our work. It meant the world to us to know that we had that support . . . we needed it desperately.

After my mom and I made it into the Charleston area that evening, we found a parking lot off to the side of the hospital. We weren't able to leave our cars there overnight, but we could for the time being, long enough to find Jimmy's room and ensure that he was all right. As I entered Jimmy's room, I saw that he was sitting up talking as the nurses were busy getting everything set up for him. They had IV medications to start, and I made sure that he got something to eat. He was starving after the reaction to his pain medicine finally subsided. After seeing that he was comfortable, my mom and I went to move my car to a parking garage, to get something to eat, and to help her find her hotel.

I find it interesting how God can put something humorous into an extremely stressful and nerve-racking situation. At the time, I was not only exhausted, I was under tremendous emotional strain as well. Top that off with two people trying to figure out directions and locate one another in a place where there are primarily one-way streets, and you have something that can be described as quite comical.

The nurses gave us what we thought sounded like easy directions from the parking lot to the parking garage. After we pulled out of the parking lot, my mother was following behind me when I noticed that she stopped at a traffic light. I called her cell phone and told her I would pull over and wait for her to catch up to me. I was driving a silver Ford Escape, and she was driving a silver BMW. As I saw the BMW drive past me, I pulled out onto the road and told my mom that I was behind her. I told her that I would stay behind her so that we wouldn't get separated, and I would tell her where she needed to turn. As we passed the first intersection, I told her to turn, but she didn't. I asked her, "Why didn't you turn?" She said, "I did turn." I didn't know what she was talking about because I was behind her and knew that she hadn't turned. I said, "I'm right behind you. Now, turn left onto the next road. I think I can get us back on track from here." She still didn't turn. She said, "I don't see you anywhere." I said, "Well, I don't know why you don't see me because I'm right behind you. Why aren't you turning when I tell you to turn??"

Just as I said that, the BMW in front of me zoomed ahead. I thought, *My mom doesn't drive like that. Oh no! I'm not following my mother!* I was following someone else the whole time and now had no idea where I was or where my mother was! Our stress level started to reach new heights. After telling her to pull over where she was, I began looking for her. As I inched across an intersection, I looked to my left and saw her parked on the side of the road. We sure were relieved to find each other! We laughed so hard until we cried.

After we finally parked my car, my mom drove us through a drive thru to get something to eat. It was after 11:00 p.m. before we checked her into her hotel room and ate dinner. We were physically, emotionally, and mentally exhausted, but I felt energy from the adrenaline. I could feel Jesus holding me up and keeping me together. My mom and I ate dinner in her room and then it was time for her to drive me back to the hospital. She dropped me off and headed back to the hotel for the night.

I entered the front of the hospital and rode the main elevator up to the tenth floor, a trip that would become all too familiar. The part of the hospital where Jimmy was staying was very nice. I was impressed by the large rooms with hardwood floors and fancy-looking furniture. By the time I got to the hospital room, it was a little after midnight, and I saw that Jimmy was resting. The nurse was busy getting his medications in order and making sure he had what he needed. I was glad to be by his side again. My heart was always where he was, and I felt like a part of me was missing when I wasn't with him.

Jimmy was thankful to be there and hopeful that we would find out why his liver was sick and how to make him well. MUSC is the medical school in South Carolina and the place in the area to go to receive the most advanced care. We would need to get used to working with the residents and the fact that this was a teaching hospital.

After helping Jimmy freshen up, I went through my suitcase to get some things to make myself as comfortable as possible. When you're staying in a hospital, you can't exactly put on your pajamas and fuzzy slippers. After brushing my teeth, I got a pillow and a blanket, curled up in the chair/bed, and did my best to get a little bit of sleep while still in my clothes. I couldn't really sleep much anyway until my nerves calmed down a little. Jimmy's parents would be arriving in the morning, and we would then be talking to the hepatologist and his team about the next plan of action.

The following morning started early with the nurses busy checking his vital signs and bringing in his medications. I showered quickly and headed to the cafeteria to grab some breakfast right before my mom got to the room. Jimmy's mom, dad, and sister arrived, and he was very comforted to see them. They hadn't seen him yet since he had been in the hospital, and I think it was a little surprising to them to see just how sick he was. He was still jaundiced and had noticeably lost some weight.

About midmorning, the hepatologist, Dr. Ira Willner, with his team of residents and students, made a seemingly dramatic entrance. We were not used to that at the smaller hospital in Greenville. But we were glad to be in their care with their level of expertise. They looked at the ultrasound pictures and told us that he did have cirrhosis of the liver. There was no obvious reason for this. He hardly ever drank alcohol, and he tested negative for all of the common liver diseases such as hepatitis A, B, or C. They told us that with the lab results of his liver being as high as they were, he would be near the top of the liver transplant list if they confirmed that he did in fact qualify for a new liver.

The doctors would need to perform a biopsy to look for a diagnosis. Considering the fact that Jimmy still had fluid in his abdomen and that his blood was not clotting like it should, they couldn't go in through his side to get the sample of liver tissue. They would have to do a transjugular biopsy, a procedure where they enter and travel through the blood vessel in the neck down to the liver. If his liver bled, it would bleed into the blood vessel instead of his abdomen. This was safer for him.

Finally, we thought, *we're getting somewhere.* We would soon have our answers and be able to move forward with a treatment. They gave him blood plasma before the procedure to help his blood clot better as a precaution. He was so tough through all of this, and I could feel the peace that the Lord was giving us. At times when I thought I would be crying, I was surprisingly calm. I couldn't let Jimmy see all of my emotions; I wanted to be strong for him.

The next day was Christmas Eve, and it was time for the biopsy. I went down with Jimmy to the area where they did the procedure. This was a minor thing, but I felt like he was going in for major surgery. I didn't want to see him have to go through this, and I always wanted to be as close to him as I could (although at times I'm sure he would have understandably preferred me to back off a little). I sat in the waiting area looking at all the other people who were also waiting on their loved ones. I would have found it interesting to hear some of their stories. I was nervous as I tried to read magazines, but that didn't help calm me. I prayed and pleaded with God to heal Jimmy.

Never before in my life had I thought about the "Footprints in the Sand" poem the way that I did during that time:

"FOOTPRINTS IN THE SAND"

One night I dreamed I was walking along the beach with the Lord.
Many scenes from my life flashed across the sky.
In each scene I noticed footprints in the sand.
Sometimes there were two sets of footprints, other times there was one only.

This bothered me because I noticed that during the low periods of my life,
when I was suffering from anguish, sorrow or defeat,
I could see only one set of footprints, so I said to the Lord,
"You promised me Lord, that if I followed you, you would walk with
me always.
But I have noticed that during the most trying periods of my life
there has only been one set of footprints in the sand.
Why, when I needed you most, have you not been there for me?"
The Lord replied, "The years when you have seen only one set of footprints,
my child, is when I carried you."
—MARY STEVENSON[2]

I could feel Jesus carrying us, providing us with the strength, peace, and grace that we needed. I felt like we were living that poem, not foreseeing how much the Lord would be bringing it to my remembrance in the months ahead.

I looked up and saw a nurse motioning for me. Jimmy's biopsy was finished and had gone very well. The only evidence that he had this done was a bandage on his neck. He was feeling okay in spite of everything, and we would hopefully have the results in a few days.

Christmas was the next day, and I started figuring out how we could make this a special day since we were going to celebrate it in the hospital. My mom and I went to the gift shop for some shopping. I bought Jimmy a book and a T-shirt, and my mom bought both of us some socks to sleep in that were quite comfortable. Something like that can really help you feel

2.   Mary Stevenson, "Footprints in the Sand," 1936, http://www.footprints-inthe-sand. com/index .php ?page=Poem/Poem.php (accessed April 7, 2011).

at home when you need it the most. I still wear those socks today and think about that Christmas every time I wear them.

The hospital was a little quieter since the doctors discharged what patients they were able to in time for the holidays. A nurse walked into the room and placed a small Christmas tree about two-feet tall on top of one of the wooden dresser-like pieces of furniture. That cheered us up. Jimmy's favorite holiday was Christmas, and he was joyful in spite of being in the hospital. We were there together, and with his parents and my stepdad arriving the next day, we were excited to be celebrating Jesus' birthday with our family. My mom and I wrapped the presents we bought in the gift shop and placed them under our little Christmas tree.

We woke up Christmas morning, and, behold, our prayers were answered! Jimmy's color was back to normal, and when the doctors came into the room, they told us that his bilirubin measurement was down to around six and a half. He felt much stronger, and this was all without a medical explanation. Mr. James and Mrs. Geneva had arrived, and my mom and stepdad were there as well. My stepfather is a radiologist, and this be-came extremely helpful to us. He knew much better than we did what questions to ask, and he was able to explain the medical terminology to us.

The results were not back yet from the biopsy, and we still didn't have a confirmed diagnosis. However, Jimmy's liver was apparently functioning better, and he would only need to stay in the hospital for a few more days. I wasn't very comfortable with leaving the hospital without more definitive answers, but Dr.

Willner assured us that they would still be monitoring Jimmy on an outpatient basis. We would be traveling back to see him once a month. We praised the Lord for this answered prayer, and we enjoyed our Christmas there in the hospital room. We opened our presents and talked about how thankful we were that Jimmy was getting better.

The following morning the nurse came into the room to weigh him and check his vital signs as they do every morning. His swelling had gone down, and I knew he hadn't been able to eat much. When he stepped on the scale that morning, it read 133 pounds. My Jimmy, at six feet tall, had lost over thirty pounds.

In preparation for our return home, the endocrinologist came to evaluate Jimmy's diabetes and teach us a better way to monitor his blood sugar. We would need to measure his food and count the amount of carbohydrates he ate. This was on top of monitoring his sodium intake to prevent him from swelling again since his liver wasn't completely healthy yet. Jimmy listened to the doctors carefully to make sure he understood all that we would need to do once we were at home. We had our challenges ahead of us, but the Lord was going to help us. And He most definitely did.

Jimmy was discharged on December 29, 2005, just in time for us to celebrate the 2006 New Year. We had been in Charleston for a week, and we were finally going home.

CHAPTER 5

Enjoying Home,
But Not for Long

(DECEMBER 2005–JANUARY 2006)

AFTER THE THREE-AND-A-HALF-HOUR DRIVE HOME, I was busy getting Jimmy's prescriptions filled and buying what groceries we needed. Shopping had to be specific because of his diet restrictions. Friends from church and our neighbors were kind to bring meals over for us. I was thankful that we would be home to celebrate the New Year, looking ahead to Jimmy's recovery and new beginnings. This was the first time that we decided to have a more serious talk about having children. I knew I was ready, and Jimmy was becoming more ready. We thought that after he was over this illness, we might plan to start our family. I sure was excited to think that having a baby could be in our near future!

I know that the Lord was helping me prepare meals after we were home. I never was that great of a cook, and now I was attempting to prepare tasteful meals without using salt. I give all the glory to God for the meals that I was able to come up with that Jimmy actually liked. They were a little bland, but not bad considering what I had to work with.

Jimmy also had to check his blood sugar and take his insulin shots more frequently because his illness made his blood sugar level difficult to control. This meant more pokes and pricks each day. Jimmy handled that better than I think anyone else could have.

Since we weren't able to do our Christmas shopping during the regular Christmas season, we planned a day to shop for some presents for our families. Jimmy enjoyed picking out gifts for his family, and he always wanted to pick out just the right thing for each person. Because we had to stick to a budget, he decided to be a little creative with what we gave to our nephews, Jacob and Jared. He thought they would each enjoy having a handmade blanket. We went to a fabric store and searched through a large selection of different patterns and colors of fleece material, finally coming to the perfect pattern for each nephew: a pattern of planets showing the solar system for Jacob (he was ten years old at the time) and a pattern showing Tigger from Winnie the Pooh for Jared (he was just one year old). Each blanket would be made of two pieces of material held together by knots around the four edges. Jimmy was thrilled about these blankets, and I enjoyed seeing him excited. That evening, Jimmy spread out the material across our living room floor and began cutting the edges for the knots that he would make around the edges of the blanket. Even though the process took a little longer than expected, he was so proud of being able to make something unique and personalized for the boys.

After New Years Day, we looked forward to Jimmy's parents staying with us for a few days. I was back to work, but Jimmy had some extra time with his family. They went to some stores and Mrs. Geneva helped me with some housework. During their stay, I learned that Jimmy was getting a new office at work. Our building had been under construction for while, and he would be moving from a cubicle to a nice office in the new area of the building. That may not seem like a big deal to some people, but I enjoyed seeing Jimmy have something to be excited and happy about after all that he had to endure. Jimmy was thrilled and ready to get back to work.

Our next plan was to drive Mr. James and Mrs. Geneva back to Hemingway and spend a few days with them. Since we stayed in the hospital during Christmas, this would be our time to celebrate the holiday with his family. We usually exchanged presents on Christmas Eve with his parents and his sister's family. It was January now, but this time was even more special because we knew what we had to be thankful for. Jimmy was no longer in the hospital, and we were all together.

The evening came on Saturday, January 7, for us to have our Christmas celebration. As we exchanged gifts, Jimmy handed me a box and told me that this was his present to me. When I opened it, a flood of emotion swept through me. It was a sculpture showing Jesus with the children (Matthew 19:14–15), which is a part of my collection of sculptures depicting the life of Christ. Since Jimmy wasn't able to do any Christmas shopping while he was in the hospital, he had asked his sister to get it for him so that he could give it to me for Christmas. Considering all that he had been through, my heart was deeply touched knowing that he did all he could to give me something so special.

After exchanging gifts, taking lots of pictures, and having lots of laughs, it was time to check Jimmy's blood sugar before bedtime. When we checked it, the meter read 296 (it needed to be below 120). *No*, we thought, *that can't be right*. He hadn't eaten anything very sweet during the day and had taken the proper amount of insulin. Lately when we checked it, it had been low, staying below 100. We measured the amount of insulin he would need to bring it down to normal and gave him the shot. This should bring it down, and we would check it again before going to bed. After about two hours, he checked it again. This time it was 320. I knew in the back of my mind that a high blood sugar level can indicate that something isn't quite right in a person's body. Sickness can hinder blood sugar control. I pushed that thought aside and figured that after taking more insulin and getting a good night's sleep, he would be doing better in the morning.

I woke up to a dark room and realized the clock read a few minutes past 3:00 a.m. As I noticed that Jimmy wasn't in the bed beside me, I heard him in the bathroom. He was throwing up again. I dug through my suitcase and found his nausea medicine in his bag full of other medications. As he sat in a chair in the kitchen, his mom walked in with a look of concern in her eyes. I had to cut his nausea pills in half so that he could take the proper dosage. As I divided the pills, his loving mother looked at me with the tenderest expression and told me that she had no idea what Jimmy would do without me. She said that she knew the Lord sent me to him. Those words penetrated my heart and gave me the support that I so dearly needed. "The Lord will give strength to His people; The Lord will bless His people with peace" (Psalm 29:11). That was just one of many times the Lord used her to give me strength.

I fished through my purse and found the card with MUSC's number on it. Dr. Willner, his hepatologist on call, called me right back, and I explained to him that Jimmy was throwing up again. Dr. Willner told me that if the nausea medicine was not working within a few hours to come straight to the emergency room. Knowing how sick Jimmy had been throughout the last month, his doctor was not taking any chances. Jimmy did not stop vomiting, and I knew we needed to leave for the hospital. *Why was this happening?* I had to stay focused.

We loaded our suitcases into our car (we knew from experience we should be prepared to stay overnight). Jimmy sat in the front seat of our car with a bag to throw up in, and his parents followed behind us in their car. Again, my adrenaline was flowing while I hung on to the Lord for help. We had to make this two-hour drive to Charleston from Hemingway while Jimmy was trying not to get sick in the car. He felt terrible and still did not complain.

I sat in the waiting area of the emergency room with Mr. James and Mrs. Geneva while the nurses escorted Jimmy back to an exam room. With the health of his liver being questionable, we knew this could be serious. After a few minutes, I went back to the exam room to be with Jimmy.

As he was lying on the bed, the nurse asked us questions. After she finished, she left the room to give the information to the doctor. Suddenly, Jimmy reached for the trash can to throw up again. I rubbed his back and wet a paper towel for him. *This can't be happening*, I thought. *Please, Lord, do we have to be in the hospital again??* This was Sunday, and I was supposed to be back to work the next day. *I'm supposed to be catching up at my job tomorrow, Jimmy is supposed to be getting better, and we are not supposed to be back in the hospital. So I'm supposed to call my boss again and tell him that I can't come into work?? This is not how it's supposed to go, Lord. I can't keep going. I'm getting weary and worn down.*

I am gracious that we have a Father in heaven Who is all-powerful. Jesus was carrying me; I couldn't keep going on my own strength. Thankfully, Jesus doesn't require us to rely on our own strength. He desires for us to rest in Him and to be sustained by His power. "He gives power to the weak, and to those who have no might He increases strength" (Isaiah 40:29). Just when I thought I was reaching the end of my rope, Jesus had a fresh, new dose of grace for me. I felt it, and I knew that with the Lord, I could keep going.

After an ultrasound tech checked Jimmy's abdomen, I walked out to the waiting area to inform his parents how he was doing. When I went back to the exam room a few minutes later, I saw that they had taken Jimmy out of the room. The nurse let me know that they took him to have an x-ray done and that they would be admitting him. I then went with Mr. James and Mrs. Geneva to eat dinner and wait on the nurse's phone call. I felt relief when they told me that he was in his room and that we could go see him. His parents helped me bring our bags to his room, and they visited with us for a little bit before heading back to Hemingway. By this time, it was about 8:00 p.m., and we didn't want them to be on the road too late into the evening. After they left for home, I tried to organize our belongings and settle down for the night. Settling down is not what happened.

As I tried to wrap my mind around the fact that we were back in the hospital *again*, I felt frustrated and alone. I grabbed my Bible and turned to Psalm 91, praying diligently for Jimmy. I was desperate and knew that nothing was more powerful than the Word of God. While the nurses were busy drawing blood, starting IV fluids, and reviewing his medical history, I paced the floor and prayed. I spoke this entire wonderful psalm of protection over Jimmy. It ends saying, "'He shall call upon Me, and I will answer him; I will be with him in trouble; I will deliver him and honor him. With long life I will satisfy him, and show him My salvation'" (Psalm 91:15–16). I held on tightly to these words and in desperation cried to God to help us.

I looked at my watch and saw that it was almost midnight. I began to notice that as the nurses asked him questions, Jimmy had a difficult time answering them clearly. He told them that he was in Greenville (we were in Charleston) and that he was born in 2006. I assumed that his liver must have taken a turn for the worse because confusion is a symptom of liver failure. *Oh no, this can't be happening.*

Suddenly multiple nurses and the resident ran into the room with urgency holding several IV bags of fluid. They told me that Jimmy had become severely dehydrated and that the dehydration was causing his confusion. The machine couldn't pump the fluid into Jimmy fast enough. They raised the IV pole as high as it would go, reached for the top of the bag, and squeezed the fluids into Jimmy. All I could do was sit, watch, and pray. After Jimmy was well hydrated, he could immediately think clearly. At this point, however, he was now weak and exhausted.

Before I could get a hold of my nerves and emotions, the resident came in to inform us that Jimmy's blood test showed that he was going into diabetic ketoacidosis (DKA). His blood sugar had been too high for a long enough period of time to change the acidity of his blood. If not strictly monitored and corrected, this can be deadly. As she told me that he would have to go to the Intensive Care Unit, the nurses were already raising the side rails of his bed to transport him.

After they wheeled Jimmy out of the room, I looked down at the floor at all of the stuff I had brought into the room. I was now by myself and had to repack all of our things and get them to our car. With Jimmy being in the ICU, there was no other place to put them. Thankfully Jimmy had one of the nicest nursing assistants assigned to him that night. She had taken care of him during his previous visit, and we had enjoyed talking to her. This sweet nursing assistant offered to help me carry our things down to the lobby. To this day, I have no idea why I didn't accept her offer. I had two pieces of luggage, the cooler with Jimmy's insulin (I had to keep it on ice), my purse, and a couple of other things. There I was at 5'1" and 100 pounds, determined that I could take care of all of that on my own. Considering that, coupled with the weight of the stress I was carrying, I'm surprised my shoulders didn't just fall off. I guess when your emotions are running high and things are happening so quickly, you don't think as logically. I know Jesus was walking along beside me carrying the weight for me.

The time was now about 3:00 a.m., and I was not about to walk out to the parking garage by myself. I stood in front of the information desk in the lobby with all of our belongings while I waited for a security guard to pick me up to take me to my car. I know I must have looked pitiful from seeing the look of sympathy on the officer's face. He loaded up our things into the trunk and drove me to my car. Even though I was not in the police car for any wrongdoing, something about riding in one still felt a bit awkward. This did wonders for my nerves. However, I couldn't have asked for a nicer and more polite officer to assist me during this highly stressful time. After unloading our things, he drove me back to the hospital. I was eager to get up to the ICU to check on Jimmy, and I hated having to be separated from him. I wouldn't have the freedom to see him anytime I wanted to like I did in a regular room.

Visiting Jimmy in the Intensive Care Unit was a new thing for me. I found my way to the waiting room and pressed the button on the intercom to let the nurse know that I was there. They told me that it would be a little while before I could come back to see him. This was difficult for me, but I had no choice—I had to wait.

There I was in the very early morning hours sitting in the waiting room looking around at the others who were there. Cell phones were plugged into outlets around the room, and people were attempting to sleep propped up in chairs. Others were awake with the look of worry on their faces. This was the first time I really talked to other people who were there for their sick loved ones as well. Finding others who were in a similar situation as I was became an enormous comfort. Even though the room was full of very different stories and situations, we were all feeling the same type of painful concern, uncertainty, and exhaustion. I was physically sitting in that waiting room, but my heart was back in the ICU.

About an hour later, a nurse walked into the room and told me I could come back to see Jimmy. *How wonderful*, I thought. I had expected I would have to wait until later in the morning to see him (it was now after 4:00 a.m.). As we walked out of the waiting room, I turned to my left and waited to enter as I watched the large automatic doors slowly pull open.

Chapter 6

Our First ICU Experience and the Days After

(January 2006)

THE NURSE LED ME THROUGH the entrance of the ICU, and I was immediately intrigued with the hustle and bustle of the medical staff. In the middle of the unit sat a large nurses' station full of computers and monitors, and the sound of constant, monotonous beeps from the medical equipment filled the area. The patients' rooms lined the outside of the unit with a small nurse's desk in front of each one, and each nurse's desk sat in front of a window that looked into their patient's room.

I felt as if I was mentally in a fog from the shock of being there as well as from the exhaustion. I was escorted into Jimmy's room and felt instant relief to see that he was okay. He was awake as the nurses worked on him, and I noticed the cluster of IV bags hanging from the pole attached to his bed. I sat in a small chair next to him and watched a monitor record his heart rate and blood pressure. The nurses explained to us which medications he needed, one of which being his insulin given intravenously.

Normally this is given with a shot, but because of his DKA, the insulin needed to be received through his IV to bring his blood sugar down quickly and to keep it down.

The nurse seemed to have trouble inserting a second IV, and she asked another nurse to help. As the second nurse began inserting the IV, a fountain of blood squirted halfway across the room. One thing I learned is that some of the events that you witness in a hospital are not for the overly squeamish. At any previous point in my life, I probably would have immediately fainted. Growing up I said that I could never be a nurse because I couldn't handle the sight of blood or anything like that. I probably couldn't have handled it then, but I sat there in the ICU amazed at the grace that the Lord was giving me. The sight of that blood hardly bothered me. Jesus gives you the measure of grace and faith that you need *when* you need it (Romans 12:3). You may think of a situation and say, "Well, I could never go through that," but the truth is that if you ever have to go through a particular circumstance, God will provide you with what you need at the time that you need it. So don't fear something because you think you couldn't handle it. Understand that "I can do all things through Christ who strengthens me" (Philippians 4:13).

Jimmy's nurse that night was very kind, and not long after I entered the room, she wheeled in a much more comfortable chair for me. I was just grateful to be with Jimmy, but this new comfortable chair was much appreciated. Jimmy talked like he was feeling better. His nausea had subsided, and the doctors were getting his blood sugar under control.

Out of nowhere, I felt a hand on my shoulder. I opened my eyes, realizing that I must have fallen asleep, and remembered where I was. That kind nurse gently woke me to tell me that I would need to go back to the waiting area. The time was around 6:30 a.m., and the nurses had to change shifts at 7:00 a.m. No visitors were allowed while they changed shifts.

As I sat in the waiting area, I knew it was time to call our families to let them know we were in the ICU. After I contacted everyone, Jimmy's parents planned to come back to the hospital that morning, and my parents happened to be in the Charleston area that day. I needed their support, and I was thankful that they were all on their way.

It didn't take long for me to realize how grungy I felt. I needed a shower badly, and all I could do was brush my teeth in the waiting area bathroom. I was used to the luxury of our having our own full, private bathroom in the regular room, but managing hygiene in the ICU waiting room was a different ballgame. I freshened up the best I could and figured I would get a shower soon enough somehow. After our parents arrived, Jimmy's mom reminded me that her brother and sister-in-law lived close by and told me that they offered for me to use their shower. How wonderful! I planned to sit with Jimmy for a little while, and then I would take them up on their offer.

A nurse came to tell me that I could go to the room to be with Jimmy. When I saw him, he seemed to be doing all right. He told me that the nurse was getting him everything he needed and that he was feeling much better. Shortly after, what looked like about fifteen doctors, residents, and students packed into

Jimmy's little room. The attending physician was one of Jimmy's hepatologists, Dr. Adrian Reuben. Even though Jimmy was in the ICU because of his diabetes, his lab results for his liver were still not what they should be. They told us that they wanted to run more tests and that Jimmy could be moved to a regular room once one became available. I was grateful that he wouldn't have to stay in the ICU and hoped we would be in a regular room by the evening.

The hospital only allowed two people to visit at a time, and I knew that Jimmy's parents were eager to see him. I stepped out after talking to the doctors and gave Mr. James and Mrs. Geneva time with Jimmy.

A little while after their visit, I walked back to the room, and the nurse informed me that they had taken Jimmy to the eye care area of the hospital for a test. I thought, *Why is he having his eyes checked?* They told me where I could find him, and I made my way through what seemed like a maze until I found where he was. He sat in a small room in a wheelchair, and I felt a little upset that I was only now getting to him. What if he had needed something? The doctors had already performed the eye test, and he was now waiting to go back to the ICU. I found out afterward that they were looking for copper deposits in his eyes because that would be a sign of Wilson's disease, a rare disease that causes damage to the liver. That would have given us a much-needed diagnosis, but that test ended up coming back negative like all of the others.

After Jimmy settled back into his hospital bed, I unintentionally started into my over-nurturing role. Jimmy was an independent man, and he did not like to be babied. I had a tendency to be over-motherly, and you can imagine how well that went over at times. While being there by his side, I must have touched a nerve, and he sharply replied back to me. I didn't want to cause him any more stress than he was already under, and I immediately got quiet instead of fussing back at him. He looked at me with a look of compassion and said, "I'm sorry for saying that." I told him that it was okay because I knew that he was going through a lot. In that tender moment, we understood that we were both having a difficult time. It was okay for us to both feel what we were feeling, and the best way to handle those times was with love and forgiveness, just like God has given us His love and forgiveness.

I learned that while I was back in the room with Jimmy, our parents had spoken with another family in the waiting area. They were the family of another patient in the ICU, a man in his forties that had been on life support for some time. He and his wife had children that were in their teenage years. His wife was just given the news that her husband's organs were failing and that he probably wouldn't survive much longer. I thought how I couldn't even imagine being in her position, not fully realizing how close I really was. I prayed for her husband and their family and thanked Jesus that Jimmy's health was improving.

When the evening grew closer, my mom and Mrs. Geneva went with me to her brother's house to shower. His name is Wallie, and his wife's name is Nancy. Their care for me during this time touched my heart dearly.

I drove all of us to their house, and after arriving I realized what an unorganized mess I had to go through to get my things out of our luggage. I was in a hurry to get back to the hospital, and trying to get my things out of four different bags didn't help me. To this day I have no idea why we had so many different pieces of luggage, but I decided it would be easiest if I just carried all of them into the house. I must have looked like I was packed to stay somewhere for a month. I was a bit frustrated, but I still had to laugh about it a little.

After my shower, I felt like a new person. I needed that mentally as well as physically. Nancy fixed me something to eat, which helped give me some strength. While I was eating, my phone rang. It was the nurse from the hospital. Jimmy was in a regular room, and she gave me his new room number.

I thanked Wallie and Nancy for their gracious hospitality toward me, and we were on our way back to the hospital. I was ready to settle in for the night and hoped to get a little bit of rest. Mr. James and Mrs. Geneva decided to go back home. My stepdad, Mike, needed to go back to Greenville, and my mom decided to stay in Charleston in a hotel in case I needed anything. Tomorrow would be a new day, and hopefully we could go home soon.

After a somewhat decent night's sleep, we woke up the next morning hoping that Jimmy's lab results would show some improvement. We anticipated what the doctors would tell us that morning, but when they came into the room, they didn't have the best news. Jimmy's bilirubin was elevated to around six, and knowing his history, they couldn't just send us home. There was potential for his liver to fail suddenly, and more serious precautions needed to be taken. Jimmy would need to begin the preliminary tests for a liver transplant because he had to be prepared for a transplant in case he suddenly needed one.

By this point in time, we weren't really shocked at the news. We had already been through so much that this didn't come as a surprise. We knew the road ahead of us could potentially be very difficult, but we would take one thing at a time with the strength and grace of God. "Are not two sparrows sold for a copper coin? And not one of them falls to the ground apart from your Father's will" (Matthew 10:29). We knew that nothing could happen to us without our Heavenly Father's say-so. By faith, we trusted in Him and knew that in some way His name would be glorified in our situation no matter what happened!

Many tests and evaluations have to take place before someone can even be considered for a liver transplant. Once the process began, we realized how extensive it was. Jimmy's heart and kidney functions had to be evaluated to make sure they could withstand the stress from the surgery. We would have to speak to a social worker so that we fully understood not only the physical but the emotional and mental stress that both the patient and the family go through. We would also have to speak with the transplant surgeon to have a full understanding of what would take place during the surgery. It all seemed like a lot to take in at one time.

The first thing that took place was our meeting with the social worker. She brought material with her that explained everything from what would happen physically with Jimmy to how to generate financial support. After her explanation, I understood why patients and their families must see a social worker before having transplant surgery. Even if everything went as it should, the recovery can cause a great deal of physical, emotional, and mental strain from everyone involved. The risk of death became very real to us.

Liver transplant surgery is the most serious of transplants because the liver is such a large organ and affects the function of so many other organs. The incision would be quite large across the abdomen, and Jimmy would be hooked up to a lot of equipment and medications. The surgery itself could take up to twelve hours or more (I had a hard enough time waiting thirty minutes for his liver biopsy to be done), and he would go to the ICU after the surgery. After Jimmy's discharge from the hospital, we would be required to live in Charleston for three months following the transplant because we would need to be close to the hospital if something were to go wrong. The cost of the transplant is hundreds of thousands of dollars, which is not covered by insurance. That is why the social worker had to talk to us about the cost and fundraising options. Families need guidance on how to raise that much money, especially when it comes to saving their loved one's life.

After the social worker left, I looked at the expression on Jimmy's face, and I can use only one word to describe it: courage. "Be strong and courageous. Do not be afraid or terrified because of them, for the Lord your God goes with you; he will never leave you nor forsake you" (Deuteronomy 31:6 NIV). He didn't let fear cripple him. He may have felt uncertain on the inside, but he didn't show it. He displayed only courage and bravery, and I assured him that I would be by his side every step of the way.

This was one of the first times the real possibility of Jimmy's life being in danger entered my mind. However, I quickly pushed that thought out of my head, and I wouldn't let my mind think that again. We would come through this because I couldn't imagine God allowing me that much heartache. I knew Jimmy had a mighty call on his life, and this would one day be a great part of his testimony.

After meeting with the social worker, we spoke with the transplant surgeon. He looked like a younger doctor, and we listened intently as he explained the actual anatomy of the surgery to us. He explained the risks and listed possible things that could go wrong. As hard as this was to hear, we had to understand what we could be walking into.

The following day my mom and Jimmy's parents were there to visit. As the four of us were coming back to the room after eating lunch in the cafeteria, we were pleasantly surprised to see the pastors of Mr. James and Mrs. Geneva's church at the time, Pastor John and Mrs. Clara, in the room visiting with Jimmy. I had always thought so much of them; they are such loving and compassionate people. They drove all the way from Hemingway to visit with Jimmy.

When it came time for them to leave, Mrs. Clara pulled me aside in the hallway. She told me that as they talked to Jimmy, they spoke with him about his relationship with the Lord. After going through a dry season spiritually in his life, Jimmy knew deep down that he needed to draw close to Jesus again. The devil had little by little pulled Jimmy's attention away from God, which can so easily happen to any of us, and before he realized it, he had distanced himself from the Lord. It is evident that Satan will try whatever sneaky tactic he can to pull our attention away from Jesus, and we must all be one hundred percent on guard against those schemes every day. "Be alert and of sober mind. Your enemy the devil prowls around like a roaring lion looking for someone to devour" (1 Peter 5:8 NIV). I thanked God for these two faithful servants whom the Lord sent to minister to Jimmy that day. He devoted his life back to Jesus, drawing close again to his life source and his strength.

Now that we had been in the hospital for nearly a week, I knew I needed to take care of things at home. Our bosses at work were very concerned and patient with our situation. Projects were backing up at my job, and I couldn't neglect everything at home. Mail had to be sorted through and bills needed to be paid. Jimmy's best friend, Thomas, planned to visit him that weekend, and we thought that would be a perfect time for me to go back to Greenville to take care of those things. We decided that Saturday I would leave to go home for a night while Thomas and his fiancée, Rebecca, spent the day with him. That way, Jimmy wouldn't be by himself. Again, I hated to leave Jimmy, but it was necessary. Besides, he was doing well and looking forward to Thomas's visit.

I left early that Saturday morning. I took my mom back home to Greenville too, and it was good that I didn't have to make the drive by myself. We arrived in the early afternoon, and I went to my work to meet with my boss for a couple of hours. After our meeting, I went home to take care of things there. I found it hard to be at home by myself not knowing if Jimmy needed me. He sounded fine on the phone, and he reassured me that I didn't need to be upset.

My heart felt heavy that evening, and the house sounded so quiet. There was a vast emptiness in the house that I could almost feel in my chest. Even though I was returning to Charleston the next morning, I felt like my being back there was an eternity away. When you feel lonely, nighttime can seem never-ending. I had to seek the Lord for comfort. I had no answers for why Jimmy and I were in this situation, but God did. So I prayed.

As I stood in my living room, I walked up to our mantel where I had the sculpture of Jesus with the children that Jimmy gave me for Christmas. As I looked at it, I saw that Jesus had two children by the hand, a boy on one side and a girl on the other. Both were looking up at Jesus, and He had both of their hands held tightly in His. However, His face was turned and looking at the girl. In my heart, I heard Jesus telling me that He is holding both of us tightly and to understand that He had His face turned toward me. Jesus was showing me that my feelings, my hurts, my fears, and my needs were not being ignored. He had His attention on me, and I was not alone. I felt His tender comfort as a tear rolled down my cheek. As Jimmy's caregiver, I couldn't express my needs to him anytime I felt like it. I had to ignore my own needs a lot of the time to be there for him. But in this moment, Jesus told me to cast all my cares on Him because He cares for me (1 Peter 5:7). By taking everything to Him, I allowed Him to nourish my soul.

Morning finally arrived, and I quickly packed our things to head back to Charleston. Jimmy's sister, Kathy, and her husband, Kenny, were visiting him that day, and I looked forward to seeing them as well. I got into Charleston around mid-morning. I parked my car in the garage and made the long walk through the brisk morning breeze to the front entrance of the hospital. I made it to Jimmy's room and saw that Kathy and Kenny were already there. We thoroughly enjoyed their being there that day, and I could tell it made Jimmy happy.

After they left that evening, Jimmy's Aunt Nancy offered to take me out to dinner. I was tremendously grateful for her kindness, and we enjoyed a nice visit and a delicious dinner that night. Afterward, I was ready to settle in for the night with my wonderful husband.

The following day was Monday, and the doctors now needed to do the evaluation of Jimmy's heart. The test that his doctor used for his heart is called a transesophageal echocardiogram. This is basically an ultrasound of the heart using a device that is placed through the mouth into the esophagus. The image produced by this ultrasound helps the doctor to evaluate different aspects of the heart. After Jimmy's doctor explained the procedure to us, the nurse came to take Jimmy to the ultrasound room. This was not a major procedure, and they told me I could be with Jimmy while he was having this done. When we arrived, the tech was friendly and welcomed me into the room. Jimmy would be awake during this, and the tech explained step by step what would take place. Jimmy had to swallow this device down into his esophagus, which was very uncomfortable for him.

The image of his heart was quite interesting to see. For the last part of the test, they injected bubbles into his heart to track the flow of blood through the four chambers. They unexpectedly found that Jimmy had a small hole in his heart between two of his chambers. This had never affected his health in the past and was probably something that was there since birth. It wasn't life threatening, but it could pose a serious problem for a liver transplant patient.

After the ultrasound, Jimmy settled back into his hospital bed, and we (my mom was there with us as well as Mr. James and Mrs. Geneva) waited to hear from his doctor. When the doctor spoke to us, he said that further evaluation of Jimmy's heart was necessary. They would have to schedule a heart catheterization. Jimmy would be awake for this procedure as well, but it would be more serious and in depth than the echocardiogram. A catheter would have to be inserted into the artery in his groin, and it would travel up the blood vessel to his heart. Dye would then be injected to provide an image of his heart's condition. His heart catheterization was scheduled for the following day.

That evening, I started feeling discouraged from all that we had been through up to that point and from wondering how long this struggle would last. Much like previous times, I felt like I was running on fumes, like I didn't have the strength to keep going. While on the phone with my close friend and spiritual mentor, Danielle, she reminded me of Ephesians 6:13, "Therefore take up the whole armor of God, that you may be able to withstand in the evil day, and having done all, to stand." God knew that I needed to talk to her at that specific time, and what she said ministered to me deeply. I felt weak, discouraged, and out of fuel, but there wasn't anything that I needed to do. I had done all I could do, and now the only thing I needed to do was stand firm in my faith. The Word of God will always strengthen and edify you, and that is exactly what happened to me that evening. I felt strengthened, edified, and renewed.

At that time, Jimmy and I were running out of clean clothes fast. When Jimmy's parents were getting ready to leave, Jimmy's mom told me that she would gladly take our clothes home, wash them, and make the trip back the following day to bring them to us. What a blessing! She brought back our clothes, smelling fresh and clean and perfectly folded. We were so thankful.

The time came for the heart catheterization, and Jimmy's mom came to the waiting area with me. The wait would be only about an hour, and we were eager to hear the outcome of this test. I was thankful to have Mrs. Geneva waiting with me. She always has such a peaceful and calm demeanor about her. After a little while, a nurse motioned for us to come back to an area to meet with the doctor. The doctor told us that Jimmy's heart looked healthy and that they didn't find any problems. Praise God! That was such wonderful news to our ears. It was now time for us to go back to Jimmy's room and wait for him to be brought back from recovery.

When the nurses brought Jimmy back into the room, he was awake, but he couldn't move very much. A large bandage was attached to the place where the catheter was inserted into his artery, and too much movement could trigger serious bleed-ing. His bed had to be at a very low incline, making eating and drinking a bit of a task. We got through that night and were eager to talk to his doctor to find out our next plan of action.

Thankfully, all the major procedures for the transplant tests were behind us. All other evaluations were just blood and urine tests. All the information from these tests was gathered and pre-sented to a board of individuals who were to decide whether or not Jimmy was a candidate for a liver transplant.

At this point, Jimmy had been in the hospital for almost two weeks, and we were ready to be home. After a few more days of recovery, the doctor told us that Jimmy's bilirubin was down to three, the lowest it had been in weeks. Again, it looked like his liver function was improving with no explanation. The board did approve for him to be on the transplant list if he came in need of one, but for now there was no longer an indication that he needed to be on the list. All the tests were not done in vain, though. We now had those taken care of in case he suddenly needed to be added to the list. With everything taken into con-sideration, they were letting us go home, and the doctors would continue to monitor him on a scheduled outpatient basis.

After that emotionally and physically draining two-week stay in the hospital, we loaded up our bags and walked down the hallway to the elevators for what we hoped would be the last time.

CHAPTER 7

Startling News and an Unforeseen Turn

(FEBRUARY 2006)

SEVERAL WEEKS WENT BY AFTER returning home, and we attempted to adjust to a new routine. I went back to work, and Jimmy spent time recovering at home. I even worked on the weekends to catch up on my job.

Jimmy was eager to have his life back to normal again. He had his new office to organize and plenty of work backed up to keep him busy for a while. The doctors told him that he could return to work but not to overdo it. After several weeks at home, Jimmy came back into the office to work on a Tuesday. He decided to work for only half days at first, which was a wise decision, and everyone in our office was extremely happy to see him.

I helped Jimmy keep track of his diet and insulin dosages at home, although he didn't really need my help. By that time, I had plenty of practice with cooking low sodium meals, and I also learned how to measure out the proper portions for his diet to help keep control of his blood sugar. We were slowly but surely figuring out our new lifestyle and how to make it work for us. We took each day at a time and hoped that Jimmy would continue getting stronger.

By the Thursday after he returned to work, Jimmy's throat began feeling sore, and I figured maybe he had picked up a virus. It became worse by Friday, and I thought it may be a good idea for him to get it checked out by his doctor before the weekend. His follow-up appointment with his liver doctor in Charleston was the upcoming Monday, but I didn't want to go through the weekend without an exam by his doctor in Greenville. His internal medicine doctor didn't see anything alarming and suggested that it was probably something that would go away on its own. Throughout Saturday and Sunday, the discomfort in his throat turned into slight pain in his chest, and by Monday morning, his pain was worse. We knew this was not going away without further medical treatment.

We were already planning to leave early on Monday for his appointment in Charleston, and Jimmy decided that we should make the drive to his appointment and let his hepatologist look into the pain he was having. As we were nearing the Charleston area, Jimmy could barely talk because the pain in his chest was almost unbearable. I made a call to the office of his hepatologist, Dr. Willner, and explained our situation to them. Dr. Willner told us that since the pain was in Jimmy's chest we would need to go straight to the emergency room instead of coming to the transplant clinic office in case there was a problem with his heart. Instead of pulling into the parking garage for the clinic, we pulled into the parking lot across from the emergency room, which we were all too familiar with.

Up to this point, this was the most pain that I had seen Jimmy endure. The fact that this pain was in his chest was a little scary. *Was it his heart? Was it something life threatening?*

Once we arrived, the nurse took us to a room right away, and she started all of the initial examinations. After asking us some questions, she drew blood for blood tests. About an hour later, the ER doctor came into the room and had some interesting and unexpected news for us. Thankfully, Jimmy's bilirubin was at a normal level, and his heart was fine. However, his white blood cell count was extremely low. Basically, he had almost no immune system, and they suspected that he had an infection in his esophagus.

The normal white blood cell count range is between 4,800 and 10,800. Jimmy's was a little over 1,000 that day. Neutrophils are a type of white blood cell, and that is the type that was low in his bloodstream. The normal range for a person's neutrophil count is between 2,400 and 8,100, and Jimmy's was about 50.

What? Why on earth would Jimmy's white blood cell count plummet? Was this connected to the sickness of his liver? Could this actually be something in addition to everything we are already dealing with? Questions raced through my mind, and I had to bring myself back into the moment. I would drive myself crazy trying to figure out the whole big picture, and I had to focus on the here and now, our next step. Even the doctor sounded baffled. And again, no answers.

Jimmy needed to be admitted to the hospital, and because of Jimmy's history, they admitted him back to the same floor he was on before, the digestive disease department of the tenth floor.

And there we were about a month after leaving the last time (it was now nearing the end of February 2006), walking down the same hall *again*. My discouragement could have crushed me if I had let it. I didn't want Jimmy to see that. I wanted to keep our focus in a positive direction. Hanging our heads down and letting our feelings take over was not going to benefit us in this situation. By the power of the Holy Spirit, I sought to keep my mind focused in the right direction. I had to for my sanity and for Jimmy's sake.

The doctor came into our room not long after we arrived, and he told us that they needed to insert a scope with a camera into Jimmy's esophagus. After that procedure, it was confirmed that he had a severe infection, and that was causing his excruciating pain. The doctors set him up on a morphine pump along with a strong oral pain medication. He was started on antibiotics, antiviral medicine, and antifungal medicine. Jimmy barely had a shred of an immune system; these medicines were his primary defense.

I had a chance to look around our room after the doctor left, and I have to say, MUSC knows how to put together nice rooms for their patients. We weren't staying in a room; we were in a suite! A doorway from the room with his hospital bed led us into a living room with nice furniture, a large TV, and a kitchenette. The furniture was old Charleston style, which I liked. If we had to be in the hospital away from home, this was the way to do it. I believed this was a way that the Lord blessed us in the midst of all that we were dealing with.

The most important thing at this point was to keep Jimmy's pain medicine from wearing off. The infection was so severe that his pain was agonizing. All he could swallow was milk, and if he tried to eat anything more solid than that he couldn't tolerate it. It would take several days for him to feel a difference from the medications, and getting through that time required tremendous endurance from Jimmy.

The following day, we were introduced to a new group of specialists, the oncologists/hematologists at MUSC. These doctors specialized in treating cancer and blood disorders. They told us that the first thing they needed to rule out was leukemia, and that would require a bone marrow biopsy. The first step in finding out what was happening to his white blood cell count was to look at a sample of his bone marrow since that is where the cells are made.

The doctor would draw a sample of the bone marrow from the back of his hip bone in the area of the lower back. We were told that the procedure would be done right there in the hospital room and that he would be awake. The area where the needle was inserted would be numb, and he would probably feel a little discomfort. But no more than when you go to the dentist to have a tooth pulled. We felt comfortable with all that the doctors explained to us, and the biopsy was scheduled for the following morning.

The next morning came, and the doctors and a nurse walked into the room with what looked like a cart carrying the tools for the biopsy. Not only were they doing this in our room, but they told me that I could sit with Jimmy as well. That was comforting to both of us. However, I felt a little nervous because I wasn't sure what to expect.

The doctor instructed Jimmy to lie on his stomach, and they uncovered the area of his lower back where the biopsy was to be taken. The nurse unfolded this blue, paper-like material and revealed the tools they were going to use. This was going to be no simple procedure (not to us anyway). I swallowed hard and attempted to prepare myself for what was about to happen next.

CHAPTER 8

More Unanswered Questions

(FEBRUARY–MARCH 2006)

I WATCHED THE DOCTOR PULL out a small syringe after they cleaned the site where the biopsy would be taken. The syringe contained the pain medicine that would numb the area. Jimmy was lying on his stomach trying his best not to show that he was nervous, and I was sitting in a chair in the corner of the room fairly close to the foot of his bed so that I wouldn't be in the way of the doctors.

The shot of numbing medicine didn't bother Jimmy much. I felt rather calm about being there for the procedure until I watched the doctor pull out what looked like a large hand tool that would come out of someone's garage. It was about a foot-long rod that had a large handle at the top. Remembering that they would have to get through the bone to extract the bone marrow, it occurred to me why such a "needle" was necessary. Thankfully, I don't think Jimmy saw the size of this thing. The doctors explained step by step to us what they were doing and began inserting the needle into the proper area.

Jimmy and I both were doing fine until the needle had to get through the bone, which is done solely by the doctor's own arm strength. As the thought of this needle going through Jimmy's bone entered my mind, I began feeling kind of funny. The procedure started getting painful for Jimmy, and he didn't hesitate to let the doctors know it. All of a sudden, in the midst of looking at the doctor hand crank this thing into Jimmy's bone and listening to the sound of Jimmy's voice, my vision went blurry and the room started getting dark. As I realized that I was in the process of passing out, I thought, *I better get out of here somehow before I become a distraction to the doctors.* I mustered up enough strength in my knees to lift myself out of the chair, discreetly walk behind the nurse, and get to the couch in our little living room. If I had not made the decision to get out of the room when I did, I would have been on the floor.

When I put my feet up on the couch, I felt sweat seeping out of every pore that I had, and I became drenched. My vision came back slowly, and after a few minutes I could sit up again. That was my first and only experience of nearly fainting in all our time in the hospital. I stood up and peeked into the room to check on Jimmy as the doctors and nurses finished up the biopsy. The procedure was much more painful than Jimmy expected it would be, and he was not happy about it.

Jimmy spent the remainder of the day and evening recovering from the biopsy, and keeping up with his pain medicine was critical. The following morning, Dr. Reuben, his hepatologist, visited us. This doctor in particular was always very serious and to the point. That morning, he asked Jimmy about the bone marrow biopsy. Jimmy didn't hesitate for a second and blurted out, "I don't know what the heck kind of dentist that doctor goes to, but that biopsy was not like having a tooth pulled!" I chuckled as I saw this serious doctor let out a laugh. I always appreciated Jimmy's boldness. He was never reluctant to say things that needed to be said whether or not it offended anyone.

Because we came to Charleston prepared to stay only one night, we didn't have much packed. After spending several days washing clothes in the bathroom sink, we needed clean clothes badly. Jimmy was fine in his hospital gown, but I couldn't go another day without getting clean clothes somehow. I decided to find the nearest Walmart in the area to get a few things. I needed comfortable clothes. I found some colorful lounge pants with matching jackets that would be perfect for wearing while sitting around in the hospital. It shows how much you're in and out of the hospital when you need a "hospital wardrobe." I wanted to look nice and be comfortable at the same time. The Lord was looking out for me because I had no idea at that point how much those clothes would be needed in the months to come.

The following morning, the oncologist/hematologist team gave us the results of the biopsy. The wonderful news was that he did not have leukemia. However, the biopsy showed that the cells that create his neutrophils were very low, and there was no explanation for that. It appeared that something was causing damage to his bone marrow, but the doctors didn't know what. So now we have something damaging his liver and his bone marrow with no answers to what it is. We were frustrated.

The oncologist/hematologist put Jimmy on what is called a neupogen injection. This is typically given to cancer patients to stimulate neutrophil production after chemotherapy wipes them out. Jimmy didn't have cancer, but he needed the medicine to help him produce these white blood cells.

The following day came with a visit from his liver doctor. Thankfully, Jimmy's liver functions were the best they had been in a long time. They were actually close to normal. His white blood cell count was still remarkably low, but the doctors explained that it would take some time for the neupogen injections to take effect. Because his immune system was still compromised, it would be safer for Jimmy to be at home instead of at the hospital. He needed to be away from other people and germs as much as possible. They were letting us go home.

After we packed our things, the nurse came into the room with a stack of nine prescriptions we needed to fill. This didn't even include the over-the-counter medications he would need. We also had a list of precautions to take to protect Jimmy from as many germs as possible. This would add to our adjustments at home, but that was okay. We were taking it one day at a time. This had been our fourth stay in the hospital (our third stay in Charleston), and after being there for about a week, we were ready to be home once again.

The time was early evening when we arrived back in Greenville, and the sun was beginning to set. We decided to go ahead to the pharmacy to fill our mountainous stack of prescriptions. When we handed them to the pharmacist, he just looked at us for a second. I guess it's not every day that someone walks in to have that many prescriptions filled at one time.

While waiting at the pharmacy, we stocked up on items that we needed to help Jimmy stay protected from germs, such as face masks and hand sanitizer. If Jimmy had to go out in public, he would need to wear a face mask that covered his nose and mouth, and he would need to use plenty of hand sanitizer even at home.

While the pharmacist was filling the prescriptions, he informed us that he didn't have the neupogen injection and that he didn't know of any pharmacy that would have it. Since this is normally administered in the hospital, he would have to special order it, and that would take days. We didn't have days. His next shot was due within the next twenty-four hours, and it was imperative that he got it on time. After getting all of our other medications, we went home and called MUSC to figure out what to do.

While waiting to hear back from the hospital, I sorted through Jimmy's medicines. He was tired, and I was glad that I could help him get it all organized. It takes organization when you have that many medications to be taken at different times throughout the day. A person could easily lose track of it all. I made a chart for him that showed each hour of the day and wrote out on the chart which medicine and how much to take when. Jimmy was thankful for my help. He felt too badly to sit and think through it all, and it was an honor for me to be his "personal assistant." After I organized his medicines, I put out our hand sanitizer and wiped down door knobs, the phones, and other surfaces with disinfectant wipes.

We finally got the call back from the hospital, and they were trying hard to get our dilemma with the neupogen shot taken care of. They contacted our hospital in Greenville and had an appointment arranged for us to go to the emergency room the following morning for Jimmy to get the shot. Knowing that Jimmy shouldn't be in a room full of people in the ER, I wasn't the happiest with this situation. I knew we would have to be very careful.

The following morning was Sunday, and after we pulled into the parking lot of the emergency room, Jimmy sat in the car while I signed him in. I explained to the nurse at the front desk about his immune system, and since MUSC called ahead for us, the hospital was prepared for us. Jimmy had to put on his face mask, and they seated us in an isolation room that had its own air flow. After a nurse came into the room and gave him the shot, we could leave; it was quite simple. This would give MUSC another day to find a pharmacy in our area that had a supply of the neupogen shots.

While at work the following day, I touched base with MUSC to find out how to get the shots. Apparently, one of the other hospitals in Greenville has a pharmacy, and I could get it from there. I felt such relief! I called the pharmacy and confirmed that they had our prescription filled. I made the thirty-minute drive through five o'clock traffic to get to the hospital. I found the pharmacy inside the hospital and quickly got in line. I was told by someone at MUSC that each shot cost about $2,000. The prescription was for ten shots, and the clerk told me that I owed $25. Praise God for health insurance! I felt like I was walking out of that hospital with a bag full of gold. I had just paid $25 for $20,000 worth of medicine.

It took us a few days to figure out how Jimmy would manage since I was going to work full time. I got up extra early in the morning and helped Jimmy get situated for the morning. This included helping him with checking his blood sugar, cooking breakfast, and helping him with his insulin shot and morning medications. That would leave me about twenty minutes to shower and get ready for work. I would then come home at lunch to help him with checking his blood sugar again, fix his lunch, and give him his lunchtime insulin shot. After work I would come straight home, and the evening was full with preparing dinner and helping him with nightly medications, one of which being the neupogen shot.

I felt very comfortable with giving Jimmy his insulin because the needle is very small, and I had a lot of practice. The neupogen shot is a different story. The needle is much larger, and much more medicine is injected. It took several times before I was good enough at it to keep from hurting him. My mom, a nurse, showed me how, and Jimmy was very patient with me. Little by little, I was learning to be a nurse myself, and I didn't mind one bit.

He got the neupogen shot once a day, but with that added to his insulin shots and his blood sugar checks, he was getting stuck with a needle about nine times a day. He was amazingly strong through this treatment.

Over the next couple of weeks, Jimmy had blood tests done at one of the Greenville hospitals to check his white blood cell count, and they would send the results to MUSC. It took only about a week for the neupogen shots to raise his neutrophil count to close to 2,000, and his doctors told us that he could stop taking the injections. Since we didn't know what caused this problem in the first place, we would have to see if his body would take over and continue making the neutrophils on its own.

Another week passed, and it was time for a follow-up appointment with Dr. Willner, his liver doctor, in Charleston. Jimmy felt stronger, and we looked forward to getting a good report from his doctor. We made our way to the waiting area, which was packed full of people, found a couple of chairs, and waited for the nurse to call Jimmy's name.

Once he was called back, the nurse first drew Jimmy's blood for lab tests, and then we were escorted to the exam room. After the exam, Dr. Willner told Jimmy that everything looked good that day and that they would continue to monitor him on an outpatient basis. We were by no means in the clear yet, but hopefully Jimmy's health would improve with time.

We stopped for lunch after the appointment and continued the drive back to Greenville. When we were about an hour and a half away from home, my cell phone rang. The voice on the other end belonged to the nurse from Dr. Willner's office at MUSC. Dr. Willner had reviewed Jimmy's lab results from that morning, and he told her to call us immediately. Jimmy's white blood cell count had plummeted once again.

CHAPTER 9

Endurance and a New Hope

(MARCH–APRIL 2006)

THE NURSE INSTRUCTED US TO start Jimmy back on the neupogen shots right away and contact his doctor in Greenville. Apparently, the shots raised his white blood cell count temporarily, but the underlying problem remained a mystery. Once we were home, I called Dr. Pugh, his internal medicine doctor, to make an appointment for the following week, and I began administering the shots again to Jimmy.

I was planning a baby shower for a close friend of mine for that upcoming Saturday, and Jimmy assured me that he felt strong enough to spare me for a few hours. The morning of the baby shower came, and Jimmy began having a low-grade fever and minor pain in his throat. He told me that he would take some pain medicine and plan to sleep most of the day and that I could still have the baby shower that I had been looking forward to for some time.

I left home feeling that Jimmy would be all right without me. I figured that if his symptoms got any worse by the time I came back, then we would consider calling his doctor. The baby shower was very enjoyable and a nice break from the gravity of all that I had been going through.

When I arrived home late that Saturday afternoon, Jimmy was sleeping in the bed feeling worse than when I had left him that morning. He had to stay on his pain medicine continuously, and he began developing some congestion. His fever was still elevated, and we knew that was a giant red flag for us. We hesitated to call his doctor because we knew they would send us to the hospital. We only wanted to go if it was absolutely necessary.

We wanted to see what happened through the night and then decide what to do if his symptoms worsened. Well, they did. By Sunday morning, his fever was up to 103 degrees, the congestion in his nose was far worse, and he could barely keep the pain in his throat at bay. We knew what we dreaded was inevitable. We got dressed and headed for the emergency room.

Because of Jimmy's weakened immune system, the nurse escorted us back to their isolation room. When she checked his temperature, it was up to 104 degrees, and I was glad we had decided to come to the hospital when we did. Jimmy felt terrible, and we had to wait through all of the evaluations from the nurses and doctors. It didn't take them long to realize how lengthy and complicated Jimmy's medical history was. It seemed like answers to all the questions in the world couldn't give them a clear enough picture of all that we had been through.

We sat in the ER for almost eight hours waiting on test results. I spent most of the time on the phone with family updating them about our situation and doing all that was in my power to make Jimmy comfortable. I knew this fever could be dangerous for him, and I tried as hard as I could to keep a positive attitude.

Finally by the time the evening came, the hospital located the correct doctor for Jimmy, and we were more than grateful for her thoroughness and expertise. She was the doctor on call for Dr. Pugh. She knew what needed to be done and did it immediately. She informed us that the best floor for Jimmy to be admitted to was the oncology/hematology floor, or the cancer floor, because nurses there are familiar with caring for patients with a compromised immune system. Once we got to the room, we noticed that everything had recently been remodeled and updated, and I had a decently comfortable place to sleep on a little mattress on the window sill. I got Jimmy settled and prepared myself to update his nurse of his complicated medical history.

Once again, God gave me amazing grace to handle my duties that were more on the gory side. Once Jimmy's IV antibiotic began working, all of the mucus that was causing his congestion had to come out. That took grace for me. Where there is a call on your life from the Lord, there is always grace to do it. And there is not only grace, but joy in doing it as well! You will find unspeakable joy in doing what pleases the Father, no matter how big or small, difficult or easy.

Jimmy continued with his neupogen shots in the hospital, and he was on more powerful antibiotics through his IV to take care of his fever and congestion. This was all a result of his low white blood cell count, and now the doctors were on a mission to figure this out. Dr. Pugh was recommending an oncologist/

hematologist in Greenville to examine his case. Jimmy's liver didn't seem to be the issue at that point, and the focus was now shifting to his immune system.

The following day was Monday, and that morning I went home to shower and pack some things for the two of us because Jimmy would need to stay in the hospital for at least several days. It was such a help to be in a hospital that is close to home, and packing was easy since I now had my "hospital wardrobe." Jimmy improved throughout the day on Monday, and we decided it would be best for me to go to work on Tuesday. Tuesday morning, I began my new schedule:

- wake up at the hospital by 6:00 a.m.
- drive home and shower
- make it to work by 8:00 a.m.
- work until 5:00 p.m.
- drive to our house to get things we needed
- pick up dinner and head straight back to the hospital for the night

I followed this schedule for the remainder of our stay. I wanted to do my part to be responsible with my job, and I also wanted to be there with Jimmy. I believe caregivers face this difficult stretch. You're being pulled on from one end to the other. You have responsibilities to others, but yet you want to be by your loved one's side.

Throughout this hasty schedule, which thankfully was only a week, my boss and coworkers told me that they were amazed at my stamina through our entire ordeal. I've always been one who is more petite in size and have never had an abundance of physical strength and energy. It's always been normal for me to need plenty of rest. I believe the fact that I had to stay strong and keep going nonstop was being used by God as a testimony of 2 Corinthians 12:10, "Therefore I take pleasure in infirmities, in reproaches, in needs, in persecutions, in distresses, for Christ's sake. For when I am weak, then I am strong." Others did not see my own strength but the Lord's.

Jimmy told me that while I was at work on Tuesday, Dr. Gluck, the new oncologist/hematologist, came by to see him. I hated that I wasn't there during his visit, but Jimmy filled me in. The next step was to draw blood for specialized tests. This would hopefully bring us closer to a diagnosis for the problem with his immune system. The blood was drawn the next day, and we would need to stay in the hospital until Jimmy could stop the IV antibiotics, which would be just a few more days. Daily lab test results showed that the neupogen shots were working again to increase his white blood cell count.

Saturday came, and the doctors were letting us go home. We had to continue the neupogen shots, and we scheduled an outpatient visit with Dr. Gluck. This appointment was about a week and a half away, and we fully anticipated hearing the results from the specialized blood tests.

The morning of the follow-up appointment came, and I hoped we would have some answers. I went to work, and Jimmy felt strong enough to go to the doctor's office by himself. I eagerly awaited the phone call from him. My phone finally rang, and the news was both frustrating and optimistic. The blood tests gave us no answers, but Dr. Gluck made the decision to send us somewhere to find some. On May 11, 2006, we were scheduled for our first appointment at Duke University Hospital.

CHAPTER 10

From a Setback to Finding Strength

(APRIL–MAY 2006)

WE FELT LIKE WE WERE finally making some progress. We weren't just stuck in this vast sea of unanswered questions. We had hope and strong optimism that the specialists and researchers at Duke University Hospital would be able to find out what was happening to Jimmy's immune system and what had happened to his liver. Were these illnesses connected? We hoped they would know.

Duke is in Durham, North Carolina, about a four-hour drive from Greenville. We looked up the information about the hospital and the specialist we would see. We did all we could think of to prepare for this visit, and we thanked God for the awesome medical expertise that would be available.

The appointment was scheduled for May 11. On Saturday, May 6, Jimmy began having pain in his abdomen and a low-grade fever. I thought, *Please, not something again.* We held off calling his doctor as long as possible, but by Sunday morning, we couldn't avoid it any longer. The symptoms were too danger-ous to ignore, and we were again headed to the hospital.

Jimmy was admitted, and when we got to the hospital room on the cancer floor, I felt like I had been worn thin. I didn't want Jimmy to see my anguish, but he must have known I was feeling that way. I prayed and begged God to bring an end to Jimmy's illness and all of these hospitalizations. *How much more could we endure?* Seeing him in pain time and time again had worn on me through the months, and I felt like I couldn't budge another inch. I wanted this to all be over. In the middle of my cry of desperation to the Lord, I heard that small voice in my heart. God spoke to me, and I heard Him say that just as a runner feels like he can't finish a race, he makes it through to the end knowing he's on the last lap. I felt like I couldn't take another step, but Jesus told me that evening that we were on our last lap. I felt strengthened. If I knew God would soon be delivering us from the grip of this sickness, then I could find enough strength to take the next step. And the next, and the next. "Let us not become weary in doing good, for at the proper time we will reap a harvest if we do not give up" (Galatians 6:9 NIV).

Jimmy was started on IV antibiotics. The neupogen shots were no longer doing as good of a job keeping his white blood cell count elevated. By the time Tuesday arrived, we were asking the doctors about his appointment on that upcoming Thursday at Duke. Dr. Gluck was out of town that week, and the doctor standing in for him seemed a bit too laidback for our comfort. He didn't quite understand the severity of our circumstances and didn't act very interested in helping us. We were frustrated and felt like we were at his mercy.

When Wednesday came, I pleaded with Dr. Pugh to help us. He was not the doctor who set up the referral for us to Duke, but he told us that he would see what he could do. The problem was that Jimmy wasn't sick enough to be transported by ambulance but too sick to be discharged from the hospital. This was a sticky situation for the doctor to figure out, but I could see the deep concern in his face.

I will always be thankful for Dr. Pugh. He went above and beyond his call of duty for Jimmy's sake that day. He stayed in contact with us that Wednesday and gave us a private number for his office so that we could reach him more directly. He contacted Duke on our behalf to see what they could do.

They decided to discharge Jimmy by 6:00 a.m. Thursday morning, and we were to drive directly to Durham, making as few stops as possible. Jimmy was desperate for a shower, and we decided to make a quick stop by our house for that and to grab our luggage (which I had already packed the night before). I helped Jimmy get ready because he was still in a lot of discomfort and quite weak, and he rested on our bed while I packed the car. I helped Jimmy into the car with our directions in hand, and as we pulled out of the driveway, we felt a strong sense of hope. I was on my way to finding out that we were indeed on our last lap.

CHAPTER 11

A New Dawn
Anticipating Health and Healing
(MAY 2006)

AS WE BEGAN OUR LENGTHY drive to Durham, I felt physically strong in spite of having little sleep from providing around-the-clock care for Jimmy. We were optimistic and full of anticipation for the care he would receive at Duke. So many other doctors couldn't find the answers that we needed, and we were glad that we still had a chance for a diagnosis. The hospital is one of the most advanced in the nation and is known for their medical research. Our conversation during the ride was light and pleasant, and I could see that Jimmy's attitude was optimistic though he was physically weak.

After the long drive, we found the front entrance of the hospital. I parked across the street and called the clinic since we didn't know exactly where to go. The receptionist gave us clear instructions, and after we found it, we made our way to the waiting area and signed in a little before noon. Everything went smoothly since they were expecting us. They called us back within fifteen minutes, and we settled into a couple of chairs in the exam room.

Dr. Murat Arcasoy, who specializes in hematology, entered the room. When he walked in, we didn't know how much he would come to deeply touch our lives. He asked us questions about Jimmy's history, which was quite lengthy by that point, and listed several possible diagnoses. We felt secure in his care and very thankful that we were there. He explained that he would need to do another bone marrow biopsy there in the clinic, and Jimmy didn't like the idea of that at all. After Jimmy explained his first experience, Dr. Arcasoy assured him that this would go much more smoothly. Jimmy didn't need to worry about being in so much pain this time around. He trusted in their care and felt reassured about the procedure.

The nurse told me that the biopsy would take less than thirty minutes and that I should wait in the waiting room. And I was perfectly fine with that because I didn't need any more fainting spells. I grabbed a couple of magazines to flip through although I didn't really read anything. I bowed my head and thanked Jesus for getting us there safely and for providing us with amazing endurance. I was there by myself with Jimmy, but just as the "Footprints in the Sand" poem says, I was far from alone.[3] Jesus was carrying me through each step we had to take.

After a little while, the nurse told me that the biopsy was finished. The waiting area had cleared out because it was nearing the end of the day. We would now need to go to another area of the clinic for Jimmy to have his blood drawn for more tests, and since he was a bit weak, I needed to push him in a wheelchair. The nurse escorted us to the area where Jimmy would have his

----

3. See note 2.

blood drawn and gave me paperwork for Jimmy to be admitted to the main hospital.

That didn't take very long, only a few minutes. I was about to find out how vast and complex the Duke University Hospital campus is, or at least it was to us. Another nurse wrote down directions (through what seemed like a maze) for how to get to a small train similar to a subway system. She told us where to take this train, and then once we exited it, how to get to the admissions office in the main part of the hospital. I felt a little intimidated, but Jimmy was just fine. Thankfully, the nurse gave us clear directions, and once we started following them, we didn't feel so lost.

As I pushed Jimmy in the wheelchair, I knew it wasn't easy for him to be so dependent. But I could sense that he was slowly pulling down his wall of independence. He had a good attitude about everything and was okay with me doing more for him. I was thankful that it didn't seem hard anymore for him to let me help him.

We turned our first corner, and I saw that I needed to push him up a rather lengthy ramp. I wasn't at all familiar with navigating someone in a wheelchair and especially not someone that's much heavier than I am. Even Jimmy had to laugh after realizing my challenge. We backed up about fifteen feet, and I gained my momentum. We were moving at a fairly nice pace when we started up the ramp, and ended up moving at a snail's pace by the time we reached the top. But we made it! We had a good laugh about that.

We followed our directions and found the area to get on the train to take to the main hospital. When the automatic doors opened, I hurriedly pushed Jimmy onto the train. Some medical personnel entered with us, pushing an empty stretcher. As the doors closed behind us, I looked up and noticed a sign that said, "Make sure all wheelchairs and stretchers are locked before departure." My first panicky thought was that I had no idea how to lock the wheelchair and that I wasn't strong enough to hold it in place. I had a mental image of Jimmy rolling all over the place. After we started moving, we found the locks. I don't know what the others there with us must have thought, but we had to laugh at that too. I thanked the Lord for helping us find the humor in these situations.

As we made our way to the main lobby of the hospital, we were in awe of how nice it was. The entryway gave us an impression that Duke cared for their patients with excellence. We would later find how true that really was. We found the admissions office, and I handed them our paperwork from Dr. Arcasoy. After we answered some questions, they told us to wait for a few minutes until they could give us the room number.

The atmosphere there was calm and peaceful. Plenty of natural light came in through the many windows of the lobby, and the sound of a piano playing filled the area. Jimmy spoke with such an optimistic attitude, and we truly felt like God had brought us there for a purpose. We both felt at peace and anticipated the end of this very long trial.

After about twenty minutes, one of the workers from the admissions department gave us our room number, directions on how to get there, and paperwork for the nurse. We were familiar enough with hospitals by then that this wasn't anything new to us.

The sun was setting just as we found our room on the ninth floor. We again were in the area with the hospital's cancer patients, and my heart felt deep compassion for all of the others there. Jimmy's nurse met us at the door of his room, and since he was already in a hospital gown, all he had to do was get in the bed. Jimmy was barely well enough for the day's trip—we both needed rest and needed it badly.

The room was much smaller than we were used to at the other hospitals. A sink was against the wall across from the foot of the hospital bed, and the bathroom with a toilet and a shower was in the corner of the room. My chair/bed was next to a large window that looked out onto the street in front of the hospital.

The nurse made sure that Jimmy got something to eat, and she was busy getting all of his medications in order. After Jimmy ate his dinner, I became aware of just how hungry I was. The time was now after 8:00 p.m. and I hadn't eaten anything since about 10:00 that morning. I needed to get our luggage and find something to eat.

After making sure that Jimmy was all right and settled, I realized that our car was still at the clinic, which wasn't too far away. The nurse told me which parking garage I needed to park in and how to get there. I found our car and drove to the garage that's across the street from the hospital. There's a train and a walkway that go underground from this garage to the hospital, and I could use either one to get to the hospital from the garage. That way, I wouldn't have to cross the street late at night.

After parking in the garage, I opened the trunk of the car and stood there for a minute figuring out how I was going to carry everything by myself. I had a small suitcase on wheels, two other small bags, our laptop case, the small cooler with Jimmy's insulin, and my purse. Again, I believe Jesus was helping me carry the weight. I strapped a bag onto the suitcase with wheels and strapped the rest onto my shoulders. I could move, although it was rather slowly. An older couple was also walking in from the garage, and I felt embarrassed about how I must have looked. They offered to help, but I figured it would be easier for me to just keep going with everything strapped to me.

I found my way to the train that runs from the garage to the hospital. I felt relieved to sit down for a moment and noticed my reflection in the window across from me. I was a sight! But that was okay. I was just ready to get our things to our room. When I exited the train, I was right in front of the main elevators (I soon found out how familiar I would become with using those elevators). When I finally got to the room, I realized we didn't have a lot of space for our things, but we made do. By that point, I definitely had worked up an appetite.

I asked the nurse where I could find something to eat. She told me that the main food in the cafeteria was no longer being served but they would have something there for me to eat. I made my way down the elevators and to the cafeteria. It was a large area, and I could see that the main places where they serve the food were closed. I looked around to see what else they had available. A few others who looked like doctors and nurses were there finding a late evening meal as well.

I looked at some refrigerated sandwiches and salads, but they didn't look appetizing to me. I then came across some cereal, and I ended up getting some Corn Pops, milk, and a little slice of pound cake. I was hungry, but my nerves were affecting my appetite. After I paid, I made my way back up the elevators to our room with my bag of food in hand. When I got back, Jimmy looked relaxed, and the nurse had him hooked up to some IV fluids. I sat down in my chair next to his bed and ate the best bowl of Corn Pops I had ever eaten!

After I ate, my stomach felt satisfied, but I felt like I needed a shower badly. I helped Jimmy get showered and freshened up first. I then unpacked my soap and shampoo in the shower. When I got into the shower, the smell of my shampoo relaxed me, and for a moment I could breathe.

I enjoyed those few minutes, but while I got dressed I heard some commotion going on in the room. I hurriedly finished in the bathroom, and when I stepped out, there were several people in the room. Two nurses stood next to a machine that was monitoring Jimmy's heart, and a phlebotomist was drawing his blood. Jimmy's potassium level was abnormal, and this could possibly affect his heart. They had to give him medication to correct it and monitor his heart. After a couple of hours, all of his levels were back to normal, and he was fine. That was enough to make me a little nervous, but I was thankful that the hospital was monitoring him so closely.

By the end of the night, I was exhausted. I had been on the phone with our families explaining how we were doing. I organized our things, and by this time it was close to midnight. Jimmy and I talked for a little bit and then he went to sleep.

The nurse brought me a couple of pillows and a blanket. My "bed" didn't recline back very far, but I made myself as comfortable as possible. My eyes felt heavy, and I found my comfort in prayer that night. I had every reason to feel alone and depressed, but I didn't feel that way. I felt God's almighty hand on us and was reassured of His presence. "Fear not, for I am with you; be not dismayed, for I am your God. I will strengthen you, yes, I will help you, I will uphold you with My righteous right hand" (Isaiah 41:10).

I didn't know what to expect the following day, but I felt like we were starting the last part of this journey. I felt full of hope for us, and I was ready to see Jimmy healthy again. I closed my eyes and drifted off to sleep.

CHAPTER 12

Settling into Our "New Home"

(MAY 2006)

I OPENED MY EYES TO see the sunrise through the window. I must have fallen back to sleep after Jimmy's early morning blood work. I decided that I wanted to shower for the day and be ready before the doctor came to the room. I hurriedly showered, dressed, and ate a little bit of breakfast from what leftovers I had from my snack the night before. Jimmy's nurse for the day came in to give him his morning medications and make sure we had all we needed. Before too long, one of his many doctors came to see us.

The doctor's name was Dr. Gockerman, and he specializes in oncology. I sensed right away that he had a strong drive to find out why Jimmy was sick and to find a treatment. The results from the bone marrow biopsy from the day before didn't really give them any new information, just that the cells that make his neutrophils were low. He listed several possible diagnoses that could explain the sickness of Jimmy's liver as well, but none of them were anywhere near confirmed.

One thing that Jimmy brought to Dr. Gockerman's attention was that his best friend, Thomas, was getting married in a few weeks, and he wanted to do whatever it took to be there. He was to be in the wedding, and he wanted to be there if at all possible. Dr. Gockerman told him with an optimistic tone of voice that he didn't see any reason at all why that would be a problem. We felt very well taken care of and sensed that no time would be wasted in getting Jimmy better. What a relief!

Not long after speaking with the doctor, an announcement was made to the patients that a hair stylist would be making his weekly visit to the patients. I thought it was absolutely wonderful to have this service available to Jimmy, especially since he had gone over two months without a haircut. At first, Jimmy wasn't too interested in it, but I convinced him that it would probably make him feel better. I signed him up, and after about thirty minutes, the barber came into the room. He told us that Jimmy wouldn't even have to get out of the bed!

He pulled out what looked like an inflatable sink, and he got the water that he needed from the faucet at the sink. I watched as he lathered Jimmy's hair and rinsed it. He then cut quite a bit of hair off and left Jimmy feeling like a new person. That made such a difference for him, and I felt better knowing that Jimmy felt better. That was an awesome blessing.

We met two other people that day that would make a huge impact on us. One of them was Paul Brown, a Patient Resource Manager. He was like an advocate for us to the hospital. He asked us a few questions and told us not to hesitate for a moment to bring a need to his attention. We thought it was wonderful to have someone like that to contact if we had a problem. He also told us about the Oncology Recreation Therapist that would be stopping by to speak with us, and we looked forward to meeting her. She was the second person that would deeply touch our lives.

About mid-afternoon on that first full day there, while Jimmy was sleeping, I made a trip to the car to unload our laundry since we had limited space in the room. When I returned, I found a stack of items which included a few word search books, a couple of other game books, and a Duke University Hospital notepad and pen. On top of the stack was a note from Kristy Everette, the Oncology Recreation Therapist. She explained in the note that she stopped by while Jimmy was sleeping and wanted to leave all of those items for us. It made a huge difference because we felt cared for. Not only were Jimmy's medical needs given attention, but his mental and emotional needs as well. I hoped she would be by again soon so we could meet her.

Later that afternoon, the doctors wanted to perform a skin biopsy. For more than a month, Jimmy had been suffering from extremely dry skin on his legs, which was a symptom of who knows what. The doctors had no idea how it even tied into all of his other symptoms, and they thought they would study a sample of his skin to see if it would give them any clues. This biopsy was very simple, and it was done right there in the room. I was grateful for their thoroughness and was glad they weren't leaving any clues uncovered.

We had a full day and felt thankful for the attentive care Jimmy was provided. The nurses even cared for me as well, and that meant a lot to me. After Jimmy ate his dinner, I went to the cafeteria to find something to eat. After dinner, it was time to settle in for the evening. Jimmy enjoyed watching cable TV in the room. That was a treat because we didn't have cable at home. I talked to our moms on the phone for a while to give them our updates. They were concerned about us, but I assured them that we were just fine.

The next morning started with a similar routine as the morning before. I woke up about sunrise and hurried through my shower before the morning visit from the doctor. When he came in, he told us that we would be changing rooms. We were currently on the 9300 hall, which is where the patients stay who have more tangible forms of cancer such as tumors and growths. They had put us there for the first two nights because there wasn't a room available on the 9100 hall, which is where Jimmy needed to be. The 9100 hall is for patients with blood-related cancers such as leukemia. That was where the doctors wanted him since Jimmy's problem was with his white blood cell count.

I wasn't very happy about us changing rooms. I practically needed a trailer to carry all of our stuff. I packed everything up and carried it with the help of his nurse. I was just starting to feel familiar with and as "at home" as possible in our little area, and now it was time to settle into a new room.

The new room number was 9122, which ended up being our little temporary home for longer than we anticipated. When we walked in, for some reason it almost felt a little more dingy than I expected, but I didn't know why I felt that way. It was the same size and layout as the other room. I just felt out of place, but I figured that maybe after a few days I would feel differently.

Then I looked at the view that we had from our window, and I saw what might be the reason God moved us to this room.

In the distance, we had the clearest, most beautiful view of the chapel at Duke University. Jimmy could see it from his bed, and he commented on how beautiful it was the way the sun was shining on it. I agreed, and that ended up being such a bright focal point for us.

In the days following, I felt that Jimmy was starting to open up a little bit about what was going on inside him. Previously, he didn't talk much about his emotions or his relationship with the Lord, and I came up against a wall every time I tried to talk to him about it. All that we had experienced up to that point must have slowly begun to soften his heart. Before he became sick, he had a few misunderstandings with some individuals at our church, and he expressed how he had forgiven them and how he wanted to have a close relationship with them again. Since quite a bit of time had passed since he attended church regularly, I sensed that he longed to be back there again. That was the Holy Spirit drawing him back, and how joyful this was to me! Our church, Redemption World Outreach Center, was a wonderful church, and all those there who knew Jimmy cared about him dearly. We were eager to get back and to be involved there together again.

The two of us had also had some painful struggles during the first two years of our marriage. Neither one of us had much of an idea of what to expect in marriage, and we both set unrealistic expectations. Even after some of those issues subsided we didn't talk about them openly. Now we were finally in a place where Jimmy felt comfortable addressing some of the problems we had. After our apologies and expressing our forgiveness, we felt refreshed and renewed. I knew in my spirit that God was dealing with us on a deeper level, both in our marriage and in our walk with Him. And if all of our sufferings with Jimmy's illness was what it took to get us to this point, it was all worth it to me. I was ready to have the three of us in our marriage again: Jesus, Jimmy, and me.

That first night in our new room was hard for me because I started to feel homesick. I felt alone and like I had no one to talk to who understood my feelings. It was late, and Jimmy was asleep. I was having one of those moments when you feel alone and like God is light-years away. As tears rolled down my cheeks, I pitifully asked Jesus to help me. I couldn't change my situation; I would have to handle it. Even though I felt like God was far away, He was speaking to me. I know it was Him who gave me the idea to list ten things that I had to be thankful for and write them down. I didn't really want to, but I knew it was needed. It didn't take long to list those ten things, and I immediately felt strong again. Having a thankful attitude can turn your perspective around in a positive direction almost instantly.

Over the next several days, we met with more doctors. Since this was also a teaching hospital, we had residents along with the attending physician. They assured us that they were working hard and as fast as they could to come up with a diagnosis and a treatment.

I will always be impressed with and grateful for the oncology nurses that took care of Jimmy. What they did was not just a job; they took care of us like we were their own family. At a time when we were far away from our home and our family, they cared for both of us emotionally as well as physically. I prayed for the Lord to bless them. They helped us at such a vulnerable and weak time. The nursing assistants were also phenomenal. We developed our own little network of friends and family, which helped us to feel more at home.

I also began to meet the families of some of the other patients. I spoke with the wife of a patient that was two doors down from us, and she helped me a lot. We shared our struggles, and I believe God used our friendship to help both of us. She was a dear lady, and I will always be grateful for her.

During the course of that first week, I developed my own daily routine. Between 4:00 and 5:00 a.m., a nurse would come in to draw Jimmy's blood for daily tests. After about an hour, another nurse would come in to check Jimmy's weight. I would struggle to open my eyes because by this point I was beyond exhausted.

Not long after that, we would usually wake up to watch the sunrise. This sight was absolutely breathtaking the way the sun would shine on the chapel with its early morning colors. Sometimes it didn't even look like we had a window—it looked like someone had hung a beautiful painting on the wall!

After sunrise, I would hurry through my shower to be ready before the daytime nurse came in with Jimmy's medications. After a few days, I was able to shorten my time for getting ready down to about ten minutes. I always liked to speak with the nurse each morning, and I was more comfortable being ready for the day before people were in and out of the room.

I kept nonperishable food from the cafeteria in the room for my breakfasts so that I could stay there and eat with Jimmy.

After breakfast, we would watch some TV or read until the doctors would come in, which would be about mid-morning. They would tell us the results of Jimmy's blood tests and describe our next plan of action, which usually included more tests. They explained the medical terminology to us in layman's terms so that we understood what was going on.

After the doctors left, the servers from the cafeteria would bring Jimmy his lunch. And since we liked to eat together, I would go down a little early to the cafeteria, pack my lunch from there, and bring it back to the room. After we ate lunch, we would rest (maybe take a nap, read a book, or make use of our game books and word searches).

By late afternoon, it was time for my daily stroll to the car to drop off our laundry that needed to be washed. I took the elevator to the bottom floor and used either the walkway or the train to the parking garage. After leaving our laundry in the car, I would ride the elevator to the main floor and get my dinner from the cafeteria. I usually made it back to the room with my dinner by the time Jimmy got his, which was around 5:00 p.m. I always wanted to bring Jimmy some food too, but I couldn't because of his diet restrictions. He had to be on a low sugar, low sodium diet with no fresh fruits or vegetables because of his neutropenia (low white blood cell count). Apparently, fresh fruits and vegetables can carry germs.

After dinner we would have a visit from the daytime nurse before the nurses changed shifts. After the night nurse took over, I helped Jimmy get ready to take a shower. I laid out his soap and shampoo in the shower and put his clean clothes in the bathroom. The nurse would unhook his IV and wrap his arm in plastic so the area wouldn't get wet. Jimmy could for the most part take care of himself, but I helped him some. While he was taking a shower, the nurse would change the sheets on his bed, and after all of that was done, he felt much better.

I then straightened the bathroom after his shower and got ready for "bed" myself. After that, we were settled and ready to go to sleep. Jimmy usually drifted off to sleep before I did, and I would try to fall asleep by 10:00 p.m.

And that was, in a nutshell, our daily routine for a while. When I had the time, I would do some work on Jimmy's laptop. The company we worked for was gracious enough to set up a way for me to work from the hospital and get paid on an hourly basis. This was a tremendous help and blessing for us. I could bring in at least a little income, and I thanked God for that.

During the week, we met Kristy, the Oncology Recreation Therapist, in person. She seemed to take a strong interest in our circumstances and became a close friend to us.

At the end of our first week, my mom came for a much-anticipated visit. We had spent hours on the phone, and her visit was like a breath of fresh air. She brought us DVDs from our church's services, books, and items from our house that we needed. Jimmy told me that he was fine with me leaving for a little bit, and we decided to go to Fuddruckers for lunch (this ended up being our weekly place for lunch). We then went to a laundry mat to wash our clothes for the week and stopped by the grocery store for some snacks and meals to keep in the room. Food from the cafeteria was getting expensive, and since we had a refrigerator in our room and a microwave on our hall, I could get some meals from the grocery store.

I enjoyed her much-needed fellowship and support. At the end of our afternoon together, she helped me take our clean clothes back to our room. After she knew we had all we needed, she left for the four-hour drive back home.

During that first week at Duke, Jimmy didn't seem to make any huge improvements, but he certainly wasn't getting worse. He was still on the antibiotics because of his compromised immune system. His white blood cell count had improved some, but not enough. However, his liver functions were staying close to normal, and we were thankful for that. The doctors were continuing to evaluate him and would soon begin more aggressive treatment. They needed to start working faster because time was not on our side.

CHAPTER 13

Spiritual Healing and Blessings

(MAY–JUNE 2006)

OUR EAGERNESS TO LEARN OF a diagnosis increased every day, and we knew the doctors were doing all they could. In the meantime, we needed to make sure our hearts were right with the One Who had our whole situation in the palm of His hand—our Heavenly Father.

I began making occasional trips to the hospital gift shop to see what they had to help pass the time. On one of my trips, I bought a pen, a notepad, and a little book that I thought Jimmy might like. The book was called *T. D. Jakes Speaks to Men* by Bishop T. D. Jakes.[4] This is a small book with one quote from Bishop Jakes on each page, totaling over 150 quotes. Jimmy had enjoyed hearing him preach in the past, and I thought maybe this would be a way for Jimmy to get back into reading and studying the Bible.

Up to this point, he had rededicated his life to Jesus. We talked about that some, but he hadn't yet started reading his Bible again.

---

4.   T. D. Jakes, *T. D. Jakes Speaks to Men!: Powerful, Life-Changing Quotes to Make You the Man God Intended You to Be!* (Minneapolis, MN: Bethany House, 1996).

My mom had brought our Bibles to us the week before. I would read mine, but I was always careful not to push too much on Jimmy. It had to be his decision to draw closer to God.

At first, he didn't seem interested in reading the book I bought him. So I decided to read through it. When I came to a quote that I found to be really powerful, I shared it with him. After a couple of days of doing this, he finally said, "Let me see that book." My heart silently leaped for joy that he was taking one more step in drawing closer to his Savior.

Soon after, he began reading his Bible regularly. He noticed the notepad and pen that I bought from the gift shop and asked if I would get him the same thing so that he could take notes as he studied God's Word. This was such a breakthrough for us. I wanted to respectfully support him, and on the inside I was doing backflips from excitement. This was a time I had waited for for almost two years.

One day after we had been at Duke for about two weeks, the nurse asked if we would be interested in having a visit from one of the chaplains. We thought that would be nice, and the nurse sent the message to the pastoral services department. That was the day that God sent us Maryland Davis, an outstanding Christian woman that was truly a vessel of God's strength for us. She came into the room, talked to us for a few minutes, and gave us a devotional to read. But the powerful moment came when she took our hands and prayed with us. As she prayed, I felt the presence of God like it was tangible. My hands felt it, and it swept through me like a wave down to my feet. I knew that the Lord was working in a powerful way. "For where two or three are gathered together in My name, I am there in the midst of them" (Matthew 18:20). He had us in our situation for a divine purpose, and even though it was hard, He revealed time and time again that He was with us, He was sustaining us, and He was working through us in ways that we weren't even aware. And He desired for us to trust Him through it all.

One of the reasons that moment was so important to me was that this was the first time Jimmy and I had prayed together in almost two years. This was something that I had longed for, and as Chaplain Davis led us in prayer, I tried to hold back my tears. I thanked Jesus from the depths of my heart for this time of prayer together, and it ended up being the beginning of something even more powerful.

After that day, I spoke with Jimmy about our daily prayer life. We had made an awesome step forward with studying the Bible together, and I asked Jimmy, "If we're expecting God for a miracle for your healing, we can't hold back on Him." It was the Lord's desire for us to be united in our faith and to come before Him in prayer. "Be anxious for nothing, but in everything by prayer and supplication, with thanksgiving, let your requests be made known to God; and the peace of God, which surpasses all understanding, will guard your hearts and minds through Christ Jesus" (Philippians 4:6–7). Jimmy agreed, and from that day forward, every morning I would sit on the side of his bed and take his hand while we bowed our heads together in prayer. What a joyous breakthrough!

One day, I was sitting on the side of his bed while he was in the bathroom. When he came out, he paused as he walked by me to get back into the bed. When he stopped, he turned toward me and put his hands on my shoulders. He then kneeled down and prayed the most amazing prayer that a husband can pray for his wife. He said, "Dear God, thank You for the forgiveness and healing that has taken place in our marriage. Thank You for my wife, who has stuck by my side through thick and thin. Help me to love her as Christ loves the church and to be the husband that You have called me to be. We praise You and worship You this day. In Jesus' Name, Amen."

I was speechless. I had never experienced such love. I knew God was allowing us to experience marriage the way that He designed it to be. And after all we had been through, I believe God was allowing us to experience the best in marriage. I didn't even know how to explain to Jimmy how much that prayer meant to me, but I think he knew without me saying anything. He got back into bed with such a sound peacefulness in his face. I held his hand and just thanked God for such a precious moment.

Also around that time, I started reading a book that would forever have an impact on my life, *90 Minutes in Heaven* by Don Piper.[5] My mom had bought the book from the gift shop at MUSC in Charleston while we were there, but I didn't think much about reading it until later. I honestly picked it up because after what seemed like hundreds of games of solitaire, I needed something else to pass the time. It's interesting how sometimes when we least expect it, God has a treasure of gold for us to uncover that we didn't even know was there. In the book, Don Piper shares his testimony of dying in a car accident, and after

5.   Don Piper and Cecil Murphey, *90 Minutes in Heaven: A True Story of Death & Life* (Grand Rapids: Revell, 2004).

ninety minutes in heaven, God brought him back to life on earth. However, that was not the part of his story that ministered to me the most. After he was brought back to life, God didn't instantly heal him from his injuries. He explained all that God brought him through while suffering from his injuries. The story is amazing, and seeing what he had to endure through his hospitalizations and recovery kept me from feeling like we were so alone in our situation. To know that someone out there understood some of the things that we were going through was especially a comfort to me.

As we began our third week there, the doctors explained that Jimmy's white blood cell count still wasn't improving, and on top of that, now his red blood cell count was decreasing. I thought, *How and why are things getting worse? Okay, God, please step in anytime now.* I held on to my faith tightly, even in the middle of my frustration. They needed to do more tests, and they told us that they wanted to see if he had lymphoma. They needed to do a small surgery to remove a lymph node from under his arm. The doctors also decided to do another liver biopsy to see what further answers they could find there. Both procedures were scheduled for the same day, and we thought that would be fine since both were relatively minor.

The day came for the procedures. The liver biopsy was done first (the same way as before by going into the blood vessel in the neck), and the removal of his lymph node was scheduled for the afternoon. Having both of those procedures done in the same day may not have been the smartest decision.

Jimmy came through both just fine, but he was completely wiped out for days.

It was after that point doctors had to tell him they didn't see any way possible for him to be well enough to leave the hospital for his friend Thomas's wedding. I knew there was no way we could go, but Jimmy was disappointed to the point of being heartbroken over it. Thomas was a groomsman for Jimmy in our wedding, and it meant a lot to Jimmy to do the same for him. But we couldn't change it. It hurt me to see the look of disappointment in his face.

Another event that happened around that time was my brother Justin's graduation from high school. I thought for sure we would be out of the hospital by that time, but we weren't. I had to tell my family that there was no way we could be there. Because we missed it, my family picked a day to come up and take me to a nice lunch. My dad and my stepmom, Sandy, came with my sister and brother. They picked me up from the hospital and treated me to Macaroni Grill for lunch. And it was wonderful! That visit meant a lot to me and helped refresh my mind.

When the results from the biopsy and surgery came back, the news was both good and bad. They didn't find any cancer, but they also didn't find any definitive answers. The only bit of information they found was that his antibodies were low. To fix this, which could possibly and theoretically treat his entire illness, they wanted to start him on what is called Intravenous Immunoglobulin (IVIG). This is an IV treatment that would supply him with antibodies, and it would be administered continuously over a few days. Even though this treatment wasn't guaranteed to work, they were at least trying something.

During the IVIG treatment, the doctors encouraged him to walk around the hall to keep strength in his legs. It wasn't easy for him, but he decided to do it. Since he had to constantly be attached to his IVs, we would have to take the IV pole with us. He put on some shoes and a jacket since he was feeling cold, and we began our walk around the hallway. He decided that he wanted a change of scenery. We turned the corner and sat on a little bench in front of the elevators that looked out over the entrance of the hospital. I saw such a sound look of contentment on Jimmy's face that day, and I felt peace that I hadn't felt before. Even though Jimmy's body was sick, his spirit was as alive as ever. The closer we are to God, the healthier we are spiritually, and that is what was happening with Jimmy. I was so in awe of what was taking place on the inside of him that it took my focus off what we were dealing with physically.

Jimmy's focus was also changing. As he looked out at two birds resting just outside the window, he asked me what my idea of ministry was. He asked if being in ministry was just preaching, or if I thought that ministry could mean other things. I told him that ministry can take on many forms. Anytime he came in contact with another person, he had an opportunity for ministry. Volunteering at church and helping someone with a need are both forms of ministry, and the possibilities are endless. He smiled and nodded. We talked about the different ways we could serve at church and how we looked forward to serving together after we went home. I longed for that experience again.

The joy in my heart could barely be contained. I praised God for this time together and anticipated what mighty works could be just around the corner.

After Jimmy recovered from the lymph node surgery and the liver biopsy and finished the IVIG treatment, the doctors wanted him to do physical therapy to keep his muscles active. They told him he needed to build up strength in case they could send us home soon (which I didn't quite see happening). At first, he was very resistant to their advice. He just didn't feel like it, which was understandable. After plenty of encouragement from all of the medical staff, he agreed. The nurse told him that a physical therapist would stop by the room and escort us to the physical therapy gym. It was hard enough for him to walk there. But he was a trooper as usual and really tried. The therapist led him through some light exercises on some of the machines before we walked back to the room.

Anytime we had a visit from someone other than a nurse or a doctor, it was revitalizing to us. We constantly stayed focused on test results and medications, and our minds welcomed the break. Almost daily we enjoyed a visit from the one who had really become more of a friend to us, Kristy, the Recreation Therapist. She was about our age, and she truly had a gift for encouraging those who were terminally ill. I especially enjoyed talking to her about what we were going through, and she always had a listening ear. She often offered to go out of her way to get us things we needed, even if it meant driving to the store. She was more than just another person on staff at the hospital; she was truly a friend who cared about us. She often seemed amazed at the endurance that Jimmy and I had, and I enjoyed sharing with her that we were one hundred percent relying on Jesus to be the source of our strength. We had many long talks about our faith, and I thanked God for bringing her to us.

Kristy's department offered some rather entertaining services for the patients at Duke. They had pet therapy that we really enjoyed, although I think I enjoyed it more than Jimmy did. Each week they would bring a trained dog around to visit us, and that was a treat for me. I always loved little animals. Jimmy didn't always want them in the room, but I would step outside the room and pet them for a little bit. There was also a lady who dressed up like a clown and would bring a cart of games around to the rooms and tell funny jokes. That was an uplifting break from the monotonous hospital care. She was kind enough to leave us a pack of UNO cards, which we really enjoyed because it was something new to do.

Our usual pastimes became reading, watching TV, playing UNO, and playing solitaire. We also had plenty of time to talk, and when Jimmy felt like talking, I was always available. One of my favorite topics of conversation was about us planning a family. In the past, Jimmy just wasn't quite ready to have children, but he was gradually warming up to the idea. We discussed having a baby after he was well and strong again. We even talked about possible baby names, which was very exciting to me. To shift our focus from our current situation to all the future held for us gave us hope and strength.

The weekly visits from my mom were also uplifting. She would bring us mail from home and other items we needed. We had our routine in place when she came: eat lunch out, do our laundry at a laundry mat, and go by the grocery store. I would stock up food in our little refrigerator that I could either eat cold or heat up in the microwave. If my stepdad was off work, he would come too. And when they weren't visiting, we had our daily talks on the phone. Even when they couldn't be there in person, they were practically there because we were giving them constant updates. It was the same with Jimmy's family. We stayed on the phone with them all the time to let them know what was happening and what the doctors were saying.

During one of my mom's visits, she was able to meet Dr. Moore, one of Jimmy's oncology doctors. To give an idea of how much my mom and I are alike, after he met her, he turned to me and said, "Well, it looks like cloning works after all!" We got such a good laugh over that!

Another person that visited was Teri Watson, one of the vice presidents at the company where we worked. She happened to already be coming to the hospital and was kind enough to bring us a bag of items from our house. Each person that came to see us or do something for us was such a comfort.

Each of Jimmy's nurses took special care of both of us. They went out of their way on more than one occasion to do things for us. One of the nurses around our age was very compassionate toward Jimmy. She told him one day that she played on a soft-ball team with the oncology department of the hospital. After he explained to her how he loved playing softball, she got the softball team to sign and write little notes to Jimmy on a softball for us to keep. I can't explain how much it meant to me to see that smile on his face.

Another kind gesture that made us feel cared for was from one of the nursing assistants. Each night when Jimmy would take his shower, I would walk down the hall to the main linen closet to get him a clean towel and washcloth. One night, I saw there were no clean washcloths. I asked the nursing assistant if she could get one for us, and after looking and not finding any, she came up with her own idea to help us. She got one of the towels and cut it up into squares for Jimmy to have a washcloth. Even that extra act of service comforted us.

This was all evidence of how God cares about every small detail of what we go through. A lot of times we think God is just way out there somewhere and that He only cares about the big stuff. But that's not the case. "Are not two sparrows sold for a copper coin? And not one of them falls to the ground apart from your Father's will. *But the very hairs of your head are all numbered.* Do not fear therefore; you are of more value than many sparrows" (Matthew 10:29–31, italics mine). If He has the hairs of our head specifically numbered, then He knows and cares about our lives down to the smallest details. We are His creation, and He loves us more than we can comprehend.

Each day carried an amount of uncertainty about Jimmy's health, and in the middle of all the physical discomforts and mental strain, I stood back in amazement as I witnessed Jimmy drawing closer and closer to Jesus. He diligently studied the Bible and took notes about what he read. We also watched services from our church on DVD. Even though we couldn't attend church, we could watch the messages together from previous Sundays.

Also, each morning I would sit on the side of Jimmy's bed, take his hand, and we would pray together. We prayed for the medical staff, for his healing, for God's will to be done through our circumstances, and most of all for the salvation of our loved ones who have not accepted Jesus to be their Savior. We thought God might use our trial to somehow bring others to Him, and Jimmy told God that he was willing to be the necessary vessel for that—how awesome! I could see God molding Jimmy's heart and doing a mighty work inside him. The more Jimmy yielded to the power of the Holy Spirit, the more solid strength I could see in him, which was the power of God.

The work that the Lord was doing inside Jimmy was beginning to be seen on the outside. Nurses would see him studying his Bible and would ask him questions. When we watched our church service DVDs, if they had a minute they would stay and watch some with us. Some of the doctors would also ask him questions about his faith, and this became an incredible ministry opportunity for him. He opened up and ministered to the hospital staff as only he could. Because of the condition that he was in, they would listen to him. I found it amazing to see this ministry at work. Jimmy was being a vessel for the Lord at times when he didn't even know it.

With all of this happening, I was in awe to see the ways that God was working in us and through us. Our marriage had been transformed, Jimmy's relationship with Jesus was restored, and now God was using our situation to display Who He is to others.

I thought, *We may not know why we are going through this, but now it is becoming evident. God has a work to do and now it is being done.*

Our breakthrough was happening. My prayer to God was, *Lord, thank You for bringing us through these trials, and thank You for the mighty work that You are doing through them. Now that this has all been accomplished, let's go ahead and wrap it all up. It's time for Jimmy's healing, and I thank You that it is coming any time now.* My assumption was that God's work had been completed. I mean, I had gotten out of it all that I wanted and all that I thought needed to be done, right? The truth was that yes, God had blessed us above and beyond what we could have expected, and I praise Him for all of that. Our sufferings had by His power yielded much fruit in our lives. However, I didn't know that He wasn't finished with us yet.

Jimmy and his friend, Thomas, at our wedding rehearsal dinner
September 5, 2003

CHAPTER 14

"Though I walk through the valley . . . I will fear no evil"

PSALM 23:4

(JUNE 2006)

OUR FIRST GLIMPSE OF GOOD news came several days after Jimmy finished the IVIG treatment. When the doctor came into the room, he gave us the news that not only had his white blood cell count elevated, but his red blood cell count had increased as well. What an answer to prayer! Maybe this treatment was working, and maybe we were gradually on the road to going back home.

At this point, we had been at Duke for about four weeks, and I was well established in my routines. One day while I was walking back to the room after heating up my lunch in the microwave, a gentleman that looked close to my parents' age stopped me in the hall. He told me that his wife had lymphoma, and she had recently been admitted. I briefly explained our story to him, and it turned out that his wife was next door to our room. He had also stayed by his wife's side all through her illness.

He told me that he had to stop and speak with me because each time he saw me I looked like a light was shining through me. He said, "Even in the middle of having to stay in the hospital, you are always smiling, and you appear almost like sunshine walking down the hall." I typically try to smile at others even if I am having a bad day, but I've never thought that I was doing anything out of the ordinary. Each day, my heart ached with the uncertainty of Jimmy's health, but God's presence must have shown through that.

I could hardly fathom what that man told me that day. Perhaps God used that as a confirmation to me that no matter how you feel, when you are continually on your face before Him, He will always be there. And sometimes ministry happens when you aren't even aware of it. It did that day. I praised the Lord for how my life could touch others even at times when I didn't realize it. Ministry doesn't just happen because of what you do or say, it happens because of who you are in Christ. God used that gentleman to encourage me, and I will always be thankful for that.

There were also a few comments made by others in the hospital that I found quite humorous. I noticed that the nurses usually wore colorful scrubs. Well, it never occurred to me that when I wore my colorful lounge pants that I blended in with the nurses. Occasionally in the cafeteria I would get stopped and asked about which floor I work on. But the funniest encounter happened when a doctor stopped me in the hallway and asked me how a particular patient was doing. It caught me off guard until I realized I was wearing my pink pants. I politely explained that I wasn't a nurse, and after he apologized, I quietly chuckled as I walked away.

Others at the hospital gave me quite a surprised look when I told them that I was with my husband in the hospital. They thought for sure I wasn't anywhere near old enough to be married. They told me that I looked like a teenager, and I proudly revealed to them that I was twenty-five. I guess with my petite stature, my hair pulled back, and very little makeup on, I really did look young. But of course I took that as a compliment. I laughed about that too.

I needed as much humor as I could get because almost a week after getting the good news about Jimmy's blood cell counts, we were confronted with bad news again. Now his red blood cell count dropped again and he needed a blood transfusion. He had never had one before, and even though this was a common thing in hospitals, it still made us nervous. After they gave us all the information about the transfusion, it was only a couple of hours before they started it. That was our first step in the direction that I didn't want to take.

The transfusion helped by giving him the red blood cells that he needed. However, a couple of days after that, while Jimmy was sitting up in the bed carrying on a normal conversation with me, he suddenly couldn't breathe. I saw the look of panic on his face, and I ran out into the hall to grab the nurse's attention. She calmly (I suppose all nurses are trained to stay calm in these situations) put the sensor on his finger to check his oxygen level. He was breathing a little bit, but it was difficult. She reclined his bed and checked his vital signs. They were all normal. After a few minutes, he could breathe again, although with some discomfort. The doctors were paged, and after doing some scans, they saw what caused it. Jimmy had suffered a pulmonary embolism, a blood clot that went to his lung. Many times if a person sits for a long time (like in a hospital bed) without much movement, a blood clot can form in a person's leg and travel through the body. It's not unlikely for it to end up in the person's lung. I had no idea at the time that many cases of pulmonary embolisms result in death. I believe the Lord spared Jimmy's life that day. It was nothing short of a miracle that he lived to see the next day.

A few days later, Jimmy's mom, Geneva, and her sister, Jody, came to spend some time with us. We couldn't wait to see them. After they arrived, we sat and talked for a little while, which was a wonderful change from our daily routine. Jimmy wasn't feeling great, but he felt better just by their being there. As we got into the later part of the afternoon, they wanted to take me out to eat. This was a treat, and after Jimmy told us that he was fine by himself for a little bit, we left.

I will never forget how just as we exited the parking garage, we were hit by one of the biggest hail storms I've ever seen. And I certainly had never driven in one. As I attempted to navigate my way to a restaurant with my windshield wipers on high, we eventually made it to a place where we wanted to eat. By the time we got there, my nerves had taken a beating. But it was all worth it. We sat down to a wonderful dinner at a steakhouse and had the most heartwarming visit. Afterward, they debated whether or not to head home or come back by the room. Since the evening was still early, they decided to come up and visit some more. And I was so glad they did.

We broke out our UNO cards and played several games while we talked and laughed. Now that was a dose of medicine that we needed! We had so much fun that night. The memory of Jimmy having that time with his mom and aunt will forever be in my memory, and I know God blessed us all that night.

I'm glad we had that wonderful memory, because had they decided to wait any longer to visit, we wouldn't have had it. A couple of days later, as Jimmy sat up in his bed, he had to cough a little bit, and as he coughed he experienced a sudden sharp pain that seemed to be near his upper back. The pain was excruciating. Jimmy always tried to hide his pain, but this time he couldn't. His nurse examined him and didn't know what caused it. We thought, *Did he somehow pull a muscle when he coughed?* But he wasn't coughing hard enough to do that, I didn't think. His doctor wanted to do a CT scan to find what in the world caused this severe pain.

They found what they thought was something called an infarct. On the scan, they saw where the blood clot that went to his lung had cut off circulation to part of his lung. This caused that tissue to actually die, and it became infected. I asked the doctor if we could have a CD of the scan to give to my stepdad, Mike, since he's a radiologist. He was planning to visit us soon, and I wanted to have his opinion.

I hated to see Jimmy in such pain. Even with pain medicine, he had a hard time sitting up, eating, and doing pretty much any basic functions. I did all I could to help him.

We then hit another problem. His digestive system began to slow down. He wasn't going to the bathroom, which was a serious problem because his body wasn't getting rid of toxins. The doctors began trying different treatments to get his digestive system moving again.

My nerves were heightened with each thing that seemed to be going wrong. The doctors couldn't give us any clear answers. The only One that I knew had the answers and had every bit of control in this situation was our Heavenly Father. I prayed and I prayed.

My mom and stepdad planned to visit us, and they knew things weren't going well. Since they're both medical professionals, this was nothing out of their comfort zone. They only wanted to help. The plan was for Mike to sit with Jimmy while my mom and I did the laundry and got groceries. Well, that didn't happen. Jimmy was such a private person, and in the middle of everything going on, he didn't want me to leave his side. I was disappointed that the day couldn't go as planned, but I understood. I stayed with him while my mom and Mike washed our laundry and bought groceries for us.

While they were away, Jimmy started feeling like he had all he could stand. I would have done anything to take his place in that hospital bed. I almost felt all that he was enduring myself, and I could hardly bear it. He was in extreme pain from the infarct, his digestive system wasn't working properly, and he was beginning to swell again around his abdomen. I sat on the side of the bed and held his hand. His nurse walked in and saw the look of complete discouragement on his face. She too sat on the

side of the bed and spoke comforting words to both of us. My
heart was crushed as I saw tears roll down Jimmy's face. I was
angry and hurt that this was happening to him, and I was helpless to stop it. I thanked his nurse for taking that special time to
be a comfort to us. I made sure Jimmy knew that not a second
would go by that I wasn't right there with him. He would not go
through a minute of this alone. That was all I could do.

After my mom and stepdad returned to the room, Mike reviewed the CT scan on the CD that we had using Jimmy's laptop.
He confirmed that Jimmy had an infarct, but there was something else he noticed that he didn't tell me until later. He could
see his liver on the scan, and it did not look good. It looked sick
and cirrhotic. He didn't want to tell us at the time because we
had so many other things to deal with, and with the blood tests
still showing that his liver functions were decent, he wanted to
spare us from more bad news that day.

As the evening grew closer, there was no sign of Jimmy's
digestive system working like it should, and the doctors wanted
to do an x-ray to see if he had an obstruction in his colon. While
we were waiting for the techs to arrive with the x-ray machine,
we had a visit from Kristy, along with one of the pet therapy
dogs, Gus, and Gus's owner, Jill Simpson. Jimmy was feeling
much too badly to have a visit from anyone, but I stepped outside the room to see them. They could see the stress in my face
and offered such words of comfort to me.

Gus was a golden retriever that would sit on your lap if you
sat on the floor. I kneeled down, and this very large but gentle
dog turned around and sat on my lap. This put a much-needed

smile on my face that evening, and I thanked them for their time with me. Jill Simpson was a special lady and offered her help if we needed it.

Soon after, the x-ray techs came to the room and did the scan. The doctors didn't see any obstruction, and we were back to square one trying to find out why his system was at a standstill. That night was difficult.

The doctors needed to somehow get the toxins out of Jimmy's body. They made the decision to insert a Nasogastric (NG) tube which would go through his nose, down his esophagus, and to his stomach. He had basically been gulping this medicine all day, and the doctors thought it would be better to slowly give him the medicine little by little through the tube. I knew they were doing all they could think of. Jimmy's condition was not a cookie-cutter, open-and-shut case. The doctors had to use their best judgment one step at a time.

They used a pediatric NG tube since it was much smaller than the adult one to keep his discomfort level at a minimum. The doctors explained how the process would go to insert the tube, and Jimmy nodded his head. He was ready to get it over with. For easier access for insertion of the tube, they had him sit in the chair next to the bed, and I stood opposite him across the room. It took three doctors, one inserting the tube, one coaching Jimmy on what to do (he had to actually swallow the tube down and needed to know when to do it), and one overseeing it all.

To say it was unpleasant would be sugarcoating it. It was awful for him. I might as well have been standing there with my hands tied behind my back because that is how helpless I felt. My heart ached. He coughed and gagged as the tube went through his nose and down his throat. The doctors hated to have him go through this on top of everything else. He was already in constant pain, swollen and completely weakened by it all. I saw it all in his eyes.

One of the doctors who was a soft-spoken lady said, "Out of all of our patients you have the most right to complain, and you just don't. I'm absolutely amazed." Now that was a powerful statement. I could only imagine the sickness they see while working with cancer patients. Her comment said two things to me: Jimmy was about as strong and courageous of a patient as you will find, and he was in a more serious condition than I realized.

After the tube was fully inserted, he was fine. Getting it in was the hard part. They connected the tube to a pump that gradually dripped the medicine into his stomach. Hopefully this would get his digestive system working properly again.

His doctors also emphasized that moving around would help his digestive system, and they told him to walk around the hall if he could. His reaction was, "Are you kidding?" He could hardly get to the bathroom. How was he supposed to walk down the hall? He agreed to give it a try.

The nurses showed him a piece of equipment that was used sort of like a walker. He could hold on to it, and it would give him much-needed support. Walking was hard, but he pushed through his discomfort anyway. I pushed the IV pole for him since he was holding on to the "walker," and we made one lap around the hall. That was all he could stand. I hoped and fully believed that even though things had gotten worse that we were on our way to recovery. Some of the looks on the nurses' faces didn't reflect my belief, but I couldn't let myself think any other way. I had to hold on to my hope.

By the following day, still nothing was happening with his digestive system, and the swelling was getting worse. The next decision the doctors made was to pull back on some of Jimmy's pain medicine. They told him to take as little as he could while they put a limit on how much he could take. Apparently, a lot of pain medicine can cause a person's bowels to slow down, and they had to take the pain medicine out of the equation. It was becoming too critical to let this go on any longer because they had to get the toxins out of Jimmy's body.

Jimmy wanted to cooperate with the doctors as best as he could, and he was determined that he could go with very little pain medicine. But the infarct was causing him the pain, and it was serious pain. I shouldn't have let him go without medicine as long as he did. It was unbearable for both of us. We were between a rock and a hard place. I couldn't stand for him to hurt like that, but we didn't want to jeopardize his digestive system either. The nurse told him that more medicine was available if he wanted it. After going all evening and half of the night in tremendous pain, he finally asked for it. He got some relief, and I believe we made the right decision. Even though the doctors weren't happy about it the following morning, we knew he needed the relief.

While things were going from bad to worse, God showed me several scriptures that helped me through it. I spent time reading through the book of Job, which shows Job's endurance through horrible circumstances and reveals the blessings he received because he endured. That helped me to understand that I could endure through our circumstances too.

Also, 2 Corinthians 4:16–18 became one of my favorite passages of Scripture during that time: "Therefore we do not lose heart. Even though our outward man is perishing, yet the inward man is being renewed day by day. For our light affliction, which is but for a moment, is working for us a far more exceeding and eternal weight of glory, while we do not look at the things which are seen, but at the things which are not seen. For the things which are seen are temporary, but the things which are not seen are eternal." First, we are not to lose heart, and that gave me strength. Second, compared to eternity (which we were created for), our light afflictions only last a moment. And they are working for us "a far more exceeding and eternal weight of glory," which gives us purpose beyond the pain we go through. Third, what we go through in these physical bodies, or in the natural, is only temporary!

Yes, we were hurting physically, mentally, and emotionally, but this part is only temporary. And this pain would yield to something much greater than we could imagine if we would not lose heart and if we keep enduring in our faith. And then God tells us not to look at these temporary afflictions, but to keep our eyes on the eternal. Stay focused, by faith, on the things that we cannot see with our physical eyes (our God, our heavenly home, and the divine purposes of our trials). Our security is not in what is tangible; it is in the eternal things that are not tangible. Hold on to that, and no situation, no matter how severe, can bring you down.

A couple of days passed after the NG tube was inserted, and there was still no sign of the medicine working. While all of that was going on, his doctors sent in an immunologist to review his case. They needed to find anyone who could give us some answers. The immunologist wanted to test for quite a few diseases and ordered to draw eleven vials of Jimmy's blood. Because of all that his veins had gone through, they couldn't draw all of them at once. Jimmy felt like a pincushion by the time it was all finished.

As the next day came, he was retaining more and more fluid. After ten days of no movement in his digestive system, I could hear the urgency in the doctor's voices. The medicine only caused his stomach to cramp fiercely with no results. They then decided to remove the NG tube.

I felt desperate. I begged and pleaded with God to step in and do the miraculous with Jimmy's health. I still believed that He would only let this go so far, but enough was enough. The Lord showed me the prayer that Jesus prayed in the Garden of Gethsemane the night before He was crucified, "He went a little farther and fell on His face, and prayed, saying, 'O My Father, if it is possible, let this cup pass from Me; nevertheless, not as I will, but as You will'" (Matthew 26:39). Even Jesus, knowing what He was about to face, still made His request to the Father. It was okay for us to do that too. Yes, our ultimate prayer was for God's will to be done. But it was okay for me to ask for a miraculous healing for Jimmy. And that's what I did. I prayed and I prayed. I begged and pleaded with God. I felt like He was another galaxy away from me, but I pressed through that and prayed with all that I had within me. My prayers were becoming frantic as my feeling of panic grew with each passing hour. We needed God to do something supernatural, and we needed it now.

It became apparent that none of the medications were working. One of the medications made him drowsy, and I didn't know at the time that the conversation we had before that medicine was administered would be our last alert conversation together. Because of his drowsiness, he wasn't able to do much on his own. Around the clock, I helped him with everything he needed. Sleep was nonexistent for me.

His swelling became worse, and one of his doctors commented that he looked like he was nine months pregnant. The swelling went into his feet and hands.

The doctors began administering the medicine that made Jimmy drowsy on the weekend beginning Saturday, June 10, 2006. By the morning of Tuesday, June 13, Jimmy started having slight trouble answering basic questions. When asked where he was, he answered that he was at Duke Hospital in Greenville, South Carolina (we were in Durham, North Carolina). This was alarming, and I knew this was possibly the result of the buildup of toxins in his body. My sense of nervousness grew, but I tried to stay calm. This was now an urgent situation; they needed to do something to fix this and do it fast.

It took all of my self-control to stay optimistic. Jimmy was in pain, swollen, and unable to move around easily. I helped him with just about everything. At times, I didn't have time to page a nurse for help. I could sense the strength of God that was with me to handle it all physically as well as emotionally. I just kept going with no hesitation.

As the day went on, his confusion became worse. Doctors and nurses were in and out all day. Hours passed and I wasn't even aware of the time. I could hardly wrap my mind around what was happening. *What was the reason for his confusion? What about getting his digestive system to work properly? We need to get him some medicine to reduce the swelling. Why is all of this happening??* They couldn't even focus on his white and red blood cell counts again until these things were taken care of. I felt like our situation was falling apart.

When evening came, some new residents whom I hadn't met before came to the room. I wanted news that was hopeful and answers to make things better. They did more blood tests, and I didn't know at the time what they had found. I asked them what they were doing to find the reason for his confusion. After telling me they scheduled an MRI that would be done that night, they paused for a second as if they were trying to find the words to say. They knew I was looking for positive feedback, but they couldn't give it to me. One of the residents was a young guy, and he just looked at me and said, "Your husband is really sick." I thought, *Of course he is! Now fix it!* My mind couldn't handle the news of what he was really trying to tell me. I wouldn't and couldn't grasp it. I couldn't accept it.

The nurse (who was a male nurse) came into the room to discuss what the doctors ordered. When he started talking to me, I had reached my breaking point. I don't think I had cried the whole time we were there, but I finally couldn't hold it in any longer. Suddenly the dam broke, and my ability to "hold it all together" was gone. Tears poured down my cheeks. By that point, Jimmy wasn't fully aware of what was happening, but I didn't want him to see me like this.

That caring nurse who I believe was assigned to us by God gave me permission to cry. I thought I was supposed to be the strong one, but he told me that it was okay for me to let it out. He told me, "Who wouldn't be crying in this situation? It's okay, and you need to allow yourself to let your emotions out." I had to. Jimmy's health had gone from bad to worse, and now I had no idea what to expect.

My crying wouldn't stop. I did all I needed to for Jimmy while tears soaked the top of my shirt. Kristy, the Recreation Therapist, stopped by and found out how serious our situation was. She offered all the support that she could.

A few minutes after she left, the nurse walked into the room with chocolate pudding in his hand. He wanted to do something even if it would only lighten my pain for a moment. He said, "My wife always says that chocolate makes a woman feel better, so I brought you some chocolate pudding. It's the only chocolate thing we had in the nurse's breakroom." I'll never forget his deep concern for us.

I knew the Lord could instantly turn things around. The doctors had limits, but Jesus doesn't. He is all-powerful and almighty. Nothing is impossible for Him, so why wasn't He step-ping in? Why hadn't He turned things around already? The only prayer I could muster up was *Jesus, help us!* My desperation grew by the minute.

That Tuesday morning, Jimmy was only a little confused. By that night, he could barely talk. My eyes stayed filled with tears as my heart ached. I called my mom and asked her to tell everyone she knew to pray for us. She made phone calls and sent emails. We needed supernatural intervention, and I know how powerful prayer is. As I tried earnestly to keep my faith strong, I could see our situation deteriorating before my eyes.

A radiology tech came at 10:00 p.m. to get Jimmy for an MRI. They needed to scan his brain to try to find a reason for his confusion. I went with him because I didn't want to leave his side. I didn't know how much he understood of what was going on, and I had to see to it that he was all right. However, I could only go so far. I had to wait outside the doors of the room where they did the scan. That is where I felt some of my worst pain yet.

I wanted them to hurry because if Jimmy got into a certain position, he would feel intense pain, and I didn't want that to happen. The techs doing the scan didn't understand that. I just wanted this to be over with. I could hear them telling him to stay still, but he couldn't. I couldn't see what they were doing, I could only hear. After about five minutes as I stood outside those large double doors, I heard him start to scream. He was screaming for me, and I couldn't get to him. I couldn't help him. I heard him yelling my name, and I couldn't get to the techs to tell them that he was probably in pain. During those few minutes that felt like an eternity, I paced the floor. I begged and pleaded with God to do something, anything. I had my hands tied, and I hated it. I hated feeling helpless. After an agonizing couple of minutes, his yelling stopped. I saw two nurses walk into the room, and a minute later, they wheeled Jimmy out. He was all right, but I felt helpless and angry.

The nurse assigned to us that night was another nurse that I believe God specifically chose for us. She helped me tremendously. She could see what I was going through and showed the deepest compassion. After we came back to the room, we encountered another problem.

After fourteen days of Jimmy's digestive system not moving, he began to vomit bile that night. Waste was backing up in his system and had to be pumped out of his stomach. The nurse taught me how to unhook him from the vacuum so that I could help him to the bathroom. And after I helped him get back into bed, I would hook him back up.

Hour after hour, he was responding less and less. I continuously tried to make him comfortable. That kind nurse was constantly in the room to help him and to comfort me. She wrapped her arms around me as tears streamed down my face.

Finally by about 4:00 a.m., she put her hand on my shoulder and told me that I had to take care of myself. I hadn't slept in almost forty-eight hours. She looked at me and said, "If you don't lay down for at least an hour, we're going to have two patients to take care of. You don't know what you may be facing tomorrow and you need the strength for it. Rest some for yourself and for

Jimmy." She knew how much I wanted to stay by Jimmy's side. She made a bed for me on a couch in a little room beside the nurse's station. She told me to lie down for at least an hour and she would schedule for nurses to take shifts to sit by Jimmy's side. After some hesitation, I agreed.

It wasn't until after I was lying down on the couch that reality started to hit me. My crying was uncontrollable, and I felt like I could hardly breathe. This was one hundred percent in God's hands. That night, while I lay there on the couch, I felt like God was galaxies away. There I was, hurting, and I couldn't feel the Lord's presence at all. Where was He and why did I feel like He was so far away? I cried to God the most desperate prayer of my life that night. *Please, God, I can't be losing Jimmy. That is not an option. He has to survive. Maybe others go through that, but not us. I can't face that. So please, please help me. Step in now. Do something, please!*

It wasn't until months later that I realized God was closer to me that night than I realized. Even though I couldn't feel Him, He was there. He spoke to me that night, and even though I couldn't hear the exact words, He spoke to my spirit, "Be still, and know that I am God" (Psalm 46:10). He quieted my troubled soul, and it wasn't until after the nurse woke me that I realized I had drifted off to sleep.

When the nurse woke me, it was about 6:00 a.m. She told me how Jimmy was doing and said that the doctors would be in soon. When I walked back into the room, his condition had worsened. He could only look at me. He couldn't talk, and he was now having trouble breathing. I called his parents and told them how things had worsened overnight. I told them to get to the hospital as soon as they could because I didn't know what we might be facing. They immediately packed their things and began their long drive to Durham.

Not long after that, his sister Kathy called and asked if things were serious enough that she and her husband, Kenny, needed to come. I told her, "Yes, come as soon as you can." I told my family the same thing, and everyone was on their way to be by our side.

Jimmy could only communicate with his eyes, and I could see that he was distressed. I talked with him and comforted him as best I could as I held his hand tightly in mine. Meanwhile, doctors were in and out of the room. First, a resident came to tell me what his blood tests revealed. That hit me hard. His liver was failing, and that was causing his kidneys to fail. I had been around long enough to know what that meant, but I couldn't let my mind even go there. Jimmy somehow had to survive this. As the resident delivered that news to me, I held my head down as tears ran down my face. I saw the look of compassion on the doctor's face. He knew how badly I was hurting.

The next doctor that came in was from the Intensive Care Unit. Jimmy was gradually having more and more trouble breathing, and I knew there was a good chance they would need to move him to ICU. He explained that Jimmy would need to be on a ventilator, and after he was placed on one there was a good chance that he wouldn't come off it. I thought, *He'll come off of it*. I told that doctor to do whatever they needed to.

The next doctor that came in was Dr. Moore, his hematologist. I could tell he was being sensitive toward me. He explained to me again what was happening to Jimmy's system. I collected my "medical knowledge" I had obtained over the previous months to come up with a question for him.

I asked, "If the doctors can get his digestive system moving, then that would get rid of his toxins, and then he could think clearly, and then he can come off of the ventilator and be fine. Now, isn't that possible??"

He didn't say much but respectfully nodded his head and said, "Yes, that's possible." I don't think he had the heart to give me more of a realistic answer, and even though I knew deep down that my idea was a stretch, I appreciated his sensitivity. I could have only handled so much at that time, and he knew that.

Maryland Davis, the chaplain, came to be with me. She prayed and read scripture with us. I desperately needed her spiritual support, and I knew she would be an awesome prayer warrior for us.

Mr. James and Mrs. Geneva were the first of our family to arrive. It was hard for them to see Jimmy in the condition that he was in. My heart ached when I saw the anguish in their faces. Mrs. Geneva's eyes filled with tears and Mr. James tried to talk to Jimmy. All Jimmy could do was look at him, and we reassured Jimmy that we were all right there with him. Shortly after they arrived, Jimmy's Aunt Jody walked into the room. She too tried to comfort him.

My dad arrived next, along with my stepmom, sister, and brother. Everyone was supporting us. My mom and stepdad were on their way.

During our family's arrival, the hepatologist (liver doctor) briefly came to speak with me. He told me that even though

Jimmy's liver was failing, he would never survive a liver transplant. That wasn't an option. There was nothing they could do.

After the doctors left the room, the nurse from the day before came to visit me. This was another way that he went above and beyond what he had to do. He kindly asked if he could bring me something to eat. I didn't feel like eating, but I decided to take him up on his offer. About forty-five minutes later, he came back with a sandwich for me. He wasn't just a fantastic nurse, he was a special person.

I believed that even though things were looking worse, God was going to rescue us anytime now. My prayers had turned into begging. I begged and begged God to help us.

Late morning, a couple of nurses hurriedly came into the room. They were there to transport Jimmy to ICU. I held his hand and kissed his cheek. One of the nurses wrote down the room number where they were taking him, and I watched as they pushed him down the hall. In that moment, I couldn't take care of him myself anymore. The feeling of having him pulled out of my reach was almost unbearable for me, but I didn't have a choice. I had to surrender my care for him to the nurses.

I turned around and looked at what had been our home for almost six weeks. Even though my corner of the room was packed full of our things, the room was completely empty without Jimmy there. But I had to stay focused. I looked at our things and thought, *How in the world am I going to pack up all of our stuff?* Our family started to help.

I reached down next to one of my suitcases and picked up a white bag. In it was Jimmy's birthday present. I had picked it up about a week earlier. Since I couldn't go far from Jimmy, I had made my way to a Duke University store on the hospital campus. Because Jimmy was quite a Duke fan, I found a Duke T-shirt and pen that I thought he would like. I planned to get him something nicer later, but I had to have something to give him on his birthday, which was only days away. I could only hold on to a strand of hope that he would be well enough to open his present on his birthday, the upcoming Saturday.

The nurse brought a cart and we packed it full. I couldn't believe how many things we had accumulated during that time. I guess we really had made it our home.

Since Jimmy was now in ICU, the only place for our things was in our car. As we walked down the hall, we happened to pass Paul Brown, the Patient Resource Manager. When I told him that Jimmy was in ICU, he told me he would help get information for some of the hotels close by. After telling him how much I appreciated that, we were on our way to the parking garage. I wanted to put everything in our car and get to the ICU to be with Jimmy as soon as possible.

As we walked down the long corridor that goes underground to the garage, we passed my mom and stepdad. They had just arrived at the hospital. I told them which floor Jimmy was on, and they decided to just meet me in the waiting room. The rest of our family helped me get our things to my car.

After unloading everything, I hurried to get to the ICU waiting room. Jimmy was on the seventh floor of the hospital. I was now running off of adrenaline. Everyone there did all they could to help me.

After entering the waiting area, our family found a place to sit while I paged the nurse's station. A woman's voice came over the speaker and told me they would be out shortly to escort me back. They were still getting Jimmy situated. I sat down nervously on the edge of a chair and gazed straight ahead. I felt utterly helpless, incapable of wrapping my mind around this horrific reality.

Duke's pet therapy dog sitting on Jessica's lap in front of Jimmy's hospital room

CHAPTER 15

Ushered into the Arms of Jesus

(JUNE 2006)

MY HEART POUNDED, AND MY mind raced through endless thoughts. My phone rang continuously with calls from friends and some of the elders at our church. The wife of Jimmy's closest friend, Thomas, called to find out what was happening. They all wanted to come to be with us.

While I waited, I managed to eat a few bites of my sandwich. Then finally the nurse appeared from around the corner to bring me back to see Jimmy.

The ICU was busy with nurses and doctors in the hallway. The room was all glass in the front, and when I walked in, I immediately hurried to Jimmy's side. I squeezed his hand and told him over and over that I was right there. I didn't know how much he understood what I said. The ventilator tube went into his mouth, and I could see that he wasn't struggling to breathe anymore. I heard the sound of air being pumped out of the machine, a sound that will forever be branded into my mind. He moved his eyes to look at me. It was a sign of response that added to my strand of hope. I found it hard to grasp how we got from where we were just days earlier to this point as my mind raced through what seemed like endless questions.

I noticed the monitors and tubes everywhere. The nurse explained that Jimmy was still initiating his breaths and that the machine was just assisting him with his breathing. He had IVs in his arms and his groin administering fluid, pain medicine, antibiotics, and other medications. Monitors recorded his heart rate and blood pressure. The sounds of it all echoed through the room. Oh, what I would have given for him to not be there.

I needed to give others a chance to see him, and after I spent some time with him, I stepped back out into the waiting room. They only allowed two visitors at a time, and I knew his parents were eager to see him. While his parents were back in the room, I had some visits from some very special people. Kristy, the Recreation Therapist, came to see me and to bring me a bag of gifts to help soothe my pain. It included a CD, a journal, and a pen. Also, some of the other nurses that took care of us the whole time as well as the families of other patients that we grew close to came to see me. We were all family by that point, and their support meant the world to me. Maryland Davis, the chaplain, also came to visit with us. Her support was dearly needed.

More of our family, including his sister Kathy and her husband, Kenny, arrived. Some of Jimmy's aunts and uncles were there as well. We were all in shock and gripped with uncertainty.

After a little while, I was able to go back and sit with Jimmy again. I talked to him, told him I loved him, and read scriptures to him. He could only look at me, and I knew that the Word of God was the most comforting and powerful thing I could say.

I didn't want him to hear distress in my voice, and I spoke as calmly as I could. I asked the nurse over and over if they knew that he was comfortable, and she assured me that he was.

I wanted so badly to know what he was feeling and thinking. I wanted to know that he wasn't afraid and to comfort him if he was. I wanted him to be able to tell me if he needed something, but he couldn't. I prayed for God to meet all of his needs. I had to have faith that where we fell short, God would step in. I just *knew* that at some point in time, Jimmy would begin to improve. Any other option wasn't possible to me.

The time was just past 6:00 p.m., and the nurses were preparing to change shifts. Since I couldn't visit during shift changes, they politely asked me to step out. I could come back after 8:00 p.m.

My family wanted me to try to eat something, and they walked with me to the cafeteria. There wasn't anything else to do.

After fixing my plate, I just sat silently and stared down at my food. I felt numb, almost paralyzed. I took a couple of bites and couldn't eat anymore. As before, my body was sitting there, but my heart was with Jimmy. I was forced to be away from him, and I hated that. I hurt from not being able to take care of him myself.

As we all made our way back to the waiting room, I sat down and flipped through pages in my Bible. That was my hope. My mind was scattered as I tried to find different verses to read. Over the last twenty-four hours, I had prayed until I was spent. What more could I pray? All I had the ability to do was sit silently before the Lord; I was exhausted.

While I waited to be back in the room with Jimmy again, Paul Brown, the Patient Resource Manager, came to see me. He handed me his card with a confirmation number written on the back. The hospital was covering the cost of two nights in the hotel across the street. I was deeply touched by this generosity. Now I knew that I had a place to stay overnight. I thanked him repeatedly and thanked the Lord for His provisions. What a blessing!

When I was able to go back to see Jimmy, Mike, my stepdad, went with me. Not long after we were in the room, the resident on call that night came in to speak with us. This was the first time in the midst of me hanging on to my hope that I was forced to mentally process the reality of our situation. The resident seemed as if he was gently trying to tell me the hard truth of what we were dealing with. Thankfully, Mike, who is a doctor himself, was there to explain it all to me. The resident said that Jimmy's liver was failing and that was causing his kidneys to fail. There was nothing they could do to reverse this. Mike then interpreted that to tell me that there was nothing medically they could do for Jimmy anymore. Medically speaking, Jimmy probably couldn't survive.

This was the first time I brought myself to ask the question I had thus far refused to ask. "How much time do you think he has left?" The doctor kindly told me that they couldn't say for sure, but possibly a few days. I swallowed hard, feeling a giant lump in my throat. I could hardly process this, feeling completely numb. I just nodded, held my head down, and wept.

Mike and the doctor stepped out to give me some time alone with Jimmy. I had already prayed all that I knew to God, and it was all in His hands now. There wasn't one thing that I could do.

I spent that precious time with Jimmy, holding his hand and just being with him. I gradually started to accept the painfully inevitable. I didn't have a choice.

I knew at that point that God had for some reason taken Jimmy's life out of the hands of the doctors. Jimmy's only chance to survive was a supernatural miracle from the Lord. And that would only happen if it was His will to do so. I wanted to make God do a miracle, but we can't make God do anything. I didn't know why God seemed so quiet. Even though I knew He was sustaining me, He just seemed so quiet. I had prayed, read, and believed the Scriptures. I did all the Bible says to do.

The only thing left I could do was commit everything to God. Jimmy was His before he was mine, and I had to be willing to commit Jimmy back to Him. I asked God to please let him stay with me. But God is sovereign, and I had to trust in Him no matter what.

The nurse let me stay a little past visiting hours that evening. Jimmy was stable, but I found it extremely hard to leave him. I stayed until almost 11:00 p.m. After thanking his night nurse for letting me spend extra time with him, I headed out to the waiting room where my mom, stepdad, and sister were waiting for me. We made the walk across the street to the hotel and checked in.

My first night away from Jimmy was painful and lonely. I wasn't complete. My sister stayed in the room with me, and after we checked in, I just sat quietly, not knowing what to think.

My parents brought stacks of mail from the house that I had to go through. Jimmy always handled our mail and our bills, and having to do it myself was a grim reminder of just how bad things were.

I figured I better do something to keep my mind focused. I sat down at the small table in the corner of the room and started writing checks for bills that were due. After I sorted through our mail, I pulled out the journal that Kristy gave me that day. I wrote down some things to see if it would help me deal with the intensity I was feeling. After a few minutes of writing, I decided to take a shower.

I wanted to go back in time and somehow keep this from happening. Being forced to walk through something you don't think you can bear is painful to the core.

My arms felt empty. After taking care of Jimmy all of this time, I now had to surrender all of the care to others. Jimmy had been ripped away from me, and I had no say in it.

After my shower, I lay in the bed feeling almost paralyzed. I just stared at the ceiling and faintly asked Jesus to help me, to help Jimmy. I closed my eyes, feeling tears roll down the side of my face. After a few minutes, I must have fallen asleep.

Visiting hours started at 8:00 a.m. the following morning. According to Jimmy's nurse (another phenomenal male nurse), they were able to get some function in his digestive system. This was a positive bit of news, and I began to feel more hopeful again.

They let me come back to be with him, and the nurse seemed very caring toward Jimmy and me. He was informative and easy to talk to. I believe the Lord set him up to be Jimmy's nurse that day.

The doctors came in for a brief visit that morning. My little bit of hope from earlier that morning soon dissipated. They told me that his red blood cell count was extremely low and that he would need another blood transfusion. I consented, of course.

Throughout the remainder of the morning and midday, Jimmy became even less responsive. He stopped looking around and soon after stopped blinking. His brain was losing function little by little. He also couldn't initiate his breaths anymore. The ventilator was now doing all the work. Then his body temperature started to drop. They wrapped him in blankets and had him under a heat lamp to keep him warm. My sadness grew hour by hour. I was totally in the arms of Jesus because I could no longer function without His help. I knew I couldn't.

About mid-afternoon, we had a visit from the doctor that stayed involved in Jimmy's case the entire time at Duke, Dr. Arcasoy. He was the first doctor that we visited there, and he seemed like a kind and caring person. When he came into the room, I saw the look of sadness on his face. I know that as a doctor, his passion and desire was to help Jimmy return home healthy again. When I walked over to thank him for all that he had done to take care of Jimmy, I saw a tear fall down his cheek. To see that kind of care in a doctor touched my heart deeply.

Not long after he left the room, I stepped out to give our family updates. While I was speaking with everyone, the nurse came out and told me that the doctors needed to speak with me. When I walked back, I met with two doctors, and one had a paper in his hand. Jimmy's bloodstream was full of toxins, and his blood needed to be cleansed. The answer to that was dialysis. They explained the risks involved, and I asked, "If we don't do dialysis, what can we expect?" Their response was, "He will probably only live for about twelve more hours." That hit me like a ton of bricks. I knew it was risky, but I signed the papers and had them start dialysis. I had to give Jimmy every fighting chance.

We continued to have more family and friends come to see him throughout the day. His close friend, Thomas, came to visit, along with another close friend, Pastor Tim. He was Jimmy's pastor when he lived in Florence, South Carolina, before moving to Greenville. They talked to him and prayed for him.

We also had visits from Jimmy's close friend Patrick and a pastor from our church, Pastor Pat. They prayed for him while we all clung to hope.

I stayed that Thursday night as long as I could just like the night before. Jimmy seemed stable even though he was now fully on the ventilator and on dialysis. I kept begging God to turn things around. I knew He could in the blink of an eye.

I returned to our hotel room that night, and my heartache went deep. My prayers were desperate. *Why are we in this situation? This happens to other people, but not us. Lord, please deliver us from this!*

My sister, Jennifer, did all she could to comfort me. About midnight, I took a shower, and while I was in there, I just kept crying out to God. After a few minutes, I got a feeling in my gut that something wasn't quite right. I got out of the shower and looked at the phone number of the nurse's station. The nurse had given me that number and told me that I could call anytime. I didn't actually think I would use it, but with the uneasiness

I felt, I decided to call. It was about 12:30 a.m., and the nurse picked up the phone.

Jimmy wasn't doing well. Because of the buildup of toxins in his body, he began having seizures. I couldn't bear the thought of not being there with him. I asked her if I needed to come in, but she told me he was stabilized and that I could probably wait until later in the morning.

A few hours later, about 4:00 a.m. on that Friday, my phone rang. It was the doctor on call that night. Jimmy was going downhill fast and I needed to come in. I again asked the question I didn't want to ask. "How much time do you think he has?" The doctor said, "It could be four hours or twenty-four hours. I'm not really sure, but you should probably come."

With shaky fingers, I dialed the numbers for the rest of our family who were also staying there in the hotel, grabbed my shoes, and started running to the hotel elevator. I just wanted to get to him. The family followed close behind as we made our way across the street to the hospital.

We couldn't go directly up to the seventh floor. Because of the time of morning, we had to go through security first. The elevator stopped on the first floor, and after getting cleared by security to be there, they allowed us up to the ICU.

My heart panicked as I anticipated what I may very soon be walking through. The nurse let all of us in the room together because of the severity of the circumstances. Jimmy was stable when we arrived, but the doctors had no way of knowing exactly how much time Jimmy had.

After a couple of hours, the nurse pulled me aside and explained that some of his medications were conflicting with each other, and they needed to know what to do. His blood pressure medicine to keep his blood pressure elevated wasn't working properly with his pain medicine. I would need to choose which medicine to keep him on. The real question was, *Do I buy him a little more time or do I keep him comfortable?* After further explanation from the doctors and from our family, I made the decision to keep him comfortable. He was so sick, and he probably wouldn't make it even with the blood pressure medicine. I just wanted to make sure he wasn't in pain.

The nurse then asked me about resuscitation. If (or when) his heart stopped, did I want them to start his heart again? All of his systems were failing. Even if they could start his heart again, it probably wouldn't last long. I decided that instead of putting him through all of that, we would just keep it more peaceful.

These are the decisions that our family had to help me make. I was in shock, complete shock. I was totally out of it trying to make the best decisions for Jimmy. I didn't even want to come to terms with all of this, much less plan for his passing. It was evident to me that the hand of God was holding me up. I couldn't have done it by myself.

The nurse gathered all of us in a room to talk to us about what to expect. I just sat still in disbelief and listened. She asked about who wanted to be with Jimmy when he passed. To see the pain in his family's eyes broke my heart. It hurt me to see them hurt.

Later that afternoon while we were all sitting with Jimmy, the resident on call asked if there was anything she could do for me. I did have one request. I wanted to wash my hair. I hadn't washed it that day, and I hated feeling so grungy. I just wanted to know if there was any place that I could do that. I didn't expect her to go out of her way, but she found a way for me to quickly wash my hair. What a blessing that something so trivial can at least bring a little bit of comfort to me.

As the evening grew near, the nurse explained that it may not be much longer. I was in agony. I couldn't hold back my weeping. Tears rolled down my cheeks and onto Jimmy's hand. I told him over and over that I loved him and that he was not alone. Our family surrounded me, but I was only focused on Jimmy, my beloved husband.

His blood pressure was dropping little by little. I looked at his hands and noticed that his fingernails were turning blue. I knew it was happening, and I couldn't deny it any longer. His skin didn't look as pink, and his hand felt cool. I just watched the monitor record his heart rate.

I stepped out for a minute to use the restroom, and when I came back into the room, I noticed something amazing. Our family was sitting around the foot of Jimmy's bed, and as I looked at his face, I found peaceful confirmation from the Lord that He was with us. Since Jimmy hadn't been able to shave, he had grown a little bit of a beard. And since his body temperature had dropped, he had a white blanket wrapped around his head for warmth. He looked like Jesus. For a moment, I didn't see the ventilator or any of the other machines. Jimmy looked like Jesus, like he was completely peaceful. I felt like God confirmed to me right then that there is divine timing in the way that He works that we cannot understand. We just need to trust Him. Jesus was letting me know that He was with us and with Jimmy.

That sweet moment still didn't take away my pain. I felt as if I was being forced to walk into my worst nightmare. I hurt beyond description. We were now getting late into Friday night, and I sat by his bed while I watched the monitor record his heart rate. It started in the 70s, then read in the 60s, then the 50s. As the night continued, Jimmy's family decided it would be too painful for them to stay. They wanted to go back to their room and for me to call them when the time came.

I did all I could to keep Jimmy comfortable. Since his mouth had to be open for the ventilator, his mouth would dry out. The nurse gave me a moisturizing swab for his mouth, and every few minutes I would wipe out his mouth. This gave me something that I could do to care for him.

We were nearing midnight, which would be June 17, 2006, Jimmy's twenty-eighth birthday. I asked my family to step out for a few minutes to give me a little bit of time alone with him. When the clock struck midnight, I leaned forward and sang "Happy Birthday" to Jimmy. I then kissed his lips for what would be the last time.

I kept telling him how much I loved him and that I will always think about him. I asked him to please always think about me too. I didn't want him to forget me. I don't know how all of that works when someone goes to heaven, but I couldn't bear the thought of him forgetting me.

After a few minutes, my family came back into the room. Jimmy's heart rate was slowly decreasing.

I felt a hand on my shoulder, and I realized that I must have dozed off. When I realized that the nurse was waking me up, I heard the alarms telling us his vitals were dropping. She said, "It won't be long." My family was sitting all around, and I looked at the monitor. His heart rate was now close to 20. My heart sank. I told him that I loved him and begged God to take me with him. *I can't do this. I can't walk through this.* I could hardly catch my breath.

I kept telling him that I loved him and that I was right there with him. His heart rate neared 10.

I looked down and noticed peacefulness in his face. In my heart I somehow new, *He's passed.* When that thought went through me, I looked up and saw his last heartbeat scroll across the monitor.

The doctor was there along with another official to pronounce him dead. At 2:40 a.m. on his twenty-eighth birthday, the doctor, after checking his pulse, just looked at me and nodded. I was so numb that tears couldn't even come at first. I just stood there.

I stepped out of the room for them to unhook Jimmy from all of the machines. Afterward, they let me back in to see him. I wondered what he was seeing, feeling, and experiencing as he was being ushered into the arms of Jesus.

CHAPTER 16

God's Faithfulness in My Deepest Despair

(JUNE–AUGUST 2006)

DISBELIEF OF WHERE I WAS and what was happening kept me from feeling the gripping pain inside my chest. As I looked down at his body, I looked at the one that I had poured out my life for. I held his lifeless hand and thought about how he was seeing things in that moment that I could only dream of imagining. He was finally healed, free from pain and in his eternal home.

As I turned around to walk out of his room, my reality slowly began to surface. My Jimmy was seeing the face of Jesus, and I now had to deal with my agony here on earth. When you're married, the fact that you're one flesh isn't to be taken lightly. My body was going through the motions, but I felt dead. The part of me that was joined with Jimmy was empty and void. I felt lost.

Jimmy's parents, sister, and brother-in-law arrived to the hospital to see him right after he passed. Mrs. Geneva shared with me how the Holy Spirit had let her know in her heart that Jimmy had gone to heaven. She had a peace that he was okay and she was not to worry. Her faith helped to provide me with comfort and strength.

The nurse told me that they would soon move Jimmy's body to the morgue and that I needed to speak with someone from the hospital's bereavement department. I kept thinking, *This isn't real. This can't be happening.* The numbness penetrated me to my core.

At that point, I just followed others' instructions. I thank God for such a supportive family because I couldn't even think for myself. The woman from the bereavement department came to the ICU waiting room to meet with me, and with the help of our family, I made hard, hard choices that no twenty-five year old should have to make.

I had to decide whether or not to have them do an autopsy. I felt extremely protective of Jimmy's body and wouldn't allow anything remotely disrespectful to happen. After explanation from her and from my stepdad, Mike, I decided it would be best for an autopsy to be performed. With the rarity of his medical condition, maybe they would find some answers that could help someone else.

They needed to know which funeral home I wanted to use. *What?* I thought. *How in the world am I supposed to know anything about that?* Facing these hard questions just kept pounding my new reality farther into my wounds.

She gave me the location and contact information for the area where Jimmy's body would be held. She was very comforting and respectful to me, and I appreciated the meticulous care from all of the hospital staff. Their excellence of care continued even after Jimmy's passing.

It was now time for us to leave the hospital, and I could barely put one foot in front of the other. My mind went into what seemed like a million directions, and the pain in my chest pounded harder and harder with every breath. The emptiness was unbearable. I wanted to go back in time. I wanted to erase where I was and what was happening.

As we (his family and mine together) exited the hospital, I could barely stand on my feet, yet I was somehow walking. The darkness of the early morning hour surrounded me. It was now about 5:00 a.m., and I felt as if with every step I walked farther into a nightmare that I couldn't avoid. Those were the hardest steps I've ever had to take. Thoughts flooded my mind. *How am I here, leaving the hospital without Jimmy? How is this possible? I'm 25 years old. Who loses a husband at 25?? What is going to be left of my life?*

I felt as if God had turned His back on us, as if He had left us behind. I couldn't even turn to Him for comfort because I was so confused. Why would God let this happen? I couldn't come up with one word to pray.

We entered the hotel, and I needed to shower and pack my things. I wanted to go back to the hospital later in the morning to speak with the nurses and doctors that had taken such good care of us for the past six weeks.

Going back to the ninth floor was difficult, and my parents went with me so I wouldn't have to go alone. This was the last place Jimmy and I had talked together, the place where we found our emotional and spiritual connection as a couple again. The shock of it all still protected me from the ever-increasing sensation of pain.

The nurses offered compassionate words of comfort to me as tears filled their eyes. I could see the sadness in the faces of the doctors as I spoke with them. They confirmed that an autopsy would be helpful to find answers. Maybe they could even find out the initial cause of Jimmy's illness.

I looked at the sun shining through the windows in the hallway, making it bright, but my heart was feeling full of darkness and sadness. The emptiness was so vast that I felt like I would just implode at any minute, making it hard to take a breath.

As we walked down that hall to the elevators, we stopped at a bench to sit down for a minute. My parents gave me the name of a recommended funeral home in Greenville, South Carolina, and they thought it would be best to give them a call. I couldn't even think for myself at that point, and I needed the guidance of others badly.

I dialed the number, and a man's voice answered. My voice was shaky and weak as I said, "I'm at Duke University Hospital in Durham, North Carolina, my husband just passed away, and I don't have any idea what I need to do." I know funeral directors are trained to speak with grieving family members, but this director comforted me more than I expected. He calmly told me step by step what I needed to do, and he assured me that they would take care of everything. I just needed to provide them with some information. His name was Christopher, and I believe God chose him specifically to handle Jimmy's funeral arrangements.

There was nothing further for me to do at the hospital. Less than twelve hours after Jimmy's passing and after weeks and months of twenty-four-hour-a-day care, all that was left for me to do was go home. My arms and my heart felt lifeless.

It was now getting close to midday, and my family helped pack my bags into my car. Since my mind was almost out of it, the plan was for my mom to ride with me and drive our car back to Greenville. She wouldn't let me make that four-hour drive back by myself, and I'm glad she didn't. I didn't need to be by myself.

The drive was quiet. I had been busy throughout the morning calling family, friends, and coworkers to let them know about Jimmy. Everyone was heartbroken, and they all reached out to help me. I made a few more calls while in the car on the way back home, but other than that, all I did was stare out the window in disbelief. I kept thinking, *This can't be real. When will I wake up from this nightmare?*

I expected pulling up in our driveway would be unbearable for me, but the shock of it all still acted as a protective shield. My parents helped unload my bags. The last time I had seen my house was the morning Jimmy and I left full of hopeful anticipation for Duke. Now I was walking back in the door alone to a house that was full of only memories. I sat in a chair in the living room with nothing to say. My disbelief of the situation kept any of it from sinking in.

My stepdad left to go home, and my mom stayed with me so I wouldn't be by myself. It wasn't until I walked into our bedroom and saw his picture that I had sitting on my dresser that even a hint of what had happened started sinking in. I grabbed his picture, held it to my chest, and fell to the floor as tears poured down my cheeks. I yelled, "Why, God, Why?! How could You turn Your back on me like this? Why did You take him? I trusted You! Jimmy trusted You! How could You?!" I felt betrayed by the One I had put all my trust in, hurt by my most Beloved Friend, Jesus. I didn't just feel the loneliness of Jimmy being gone, but I felt dismissed by the One that is supposed to be closer than anything. Jesus was my Love, and the hurt that I felt from Him not answering the most critical of my prayers ran deeper than I could comprehend.

I felt as if I not only lost my husband but my relationship with Jesus, the One Who I had been able to run to my whole life. I felt so hurt by Him that I didn't want to ask Him for help anymore. That only multiplied my emptiness.

Even though I felt hurt by God, He understood what I was going through. And even though I couldn't bring myself to ask Him for help, He was helping me. Every breath I breathed and every step I took was given to me by Him. The strength to go from one minute to the next came from Him. Even when we don't have the ability to pray or to ask Him for what we need, He is faithful. Psalm 34:18 says, "The Lord is close to the brokenhearted and saves those who are crushed in spirit" (NIV). The love of Jesus reaches far beyond our temporary hurts and feelings. No matter what type of hurt you experience, He is close to you because He loves you more than you can imagine.

My mom didn't want me to be alone, and she decided to stay with me for a week after coming home. There were a lot of things to deal with, like our finances and planning the funeral. I didn't even know where to start. Every time I turned around

I was faced with something that Jimmy always took care of, and now I had to figure it out. It was all one reminder after another that Jimmy wasn't there to help me. He took care of me in so many ways and I had absolutely no idea how I was going to make it on my own.

I stayed in shock that first night home. I wanted so badly to grab a hold of anything that could provide something tangible of Jimmy. My mom wanted us to come home to a clean house, and she had cleaned and washed all of our laundry that we left behind while we were at Duke. I appreciated her help, but this left me with not one thing that I could hold that Jimmy had worn. I buried my face in his hats to get even a hint of his scent. Jimmy not being with me just couldn't be real. It wasn't right.

The next morning, I had an appointment to meet with Christopher, the funeral director. Almost like a robot doing what it's programmed to do, I got dressed that morning and rode with my mom and stepdad to the funeral home. They practically had to be my mind because I couldn't think, let alone make important decisions. Christopher guided us through each step. We had to provide information for the obituary section of the newspapers. While we sat at the table discussing this, Christopher mentioned my being a widow. For the last thirty-six hours I had felt as if I no longer had an identity. Was I no longer a wife? I couldn't just consider myself single again. Who was I? At that moment it occurred to me that I did have an identity after all. I was a widow. For some reason, that consoled me.

Christopher continued to explain the process of planning the funeral. One thing that was an absolute top priority for me was that Jimmy be treated with the highest level of dignity. He assured me that they operated no other way, and he promised to let me know when they were bringing Jimmy to the funeral home. I had been in contact with the hospital to know exactly where his body was and when the autopsy was done. I had to know. I was still taking care of him. I was still his caregiver.

The most painful part of that day was when we were escorted into the room to select Jimmy's casket. Reality sank in much deeper at that point, and still the shock protected me from feeling the harsh blows. I thought, *This can't be real.* I wanted Jimmy to have the best and the finest. I picked one that I thought he would have liked. When we finished our meeting that day, I felt like I had planned a burial for Jimmy that would give him the respect and honor he deserved.

Next, we met with the church to go over details of the funeral service. It was held at our church, Redemption World Outreach Center, in Greenville, South Carolina. Our dear friends Patrick and Danielle did a lot to help me. Patrick was on staff at the church, and especially since he and Jimmy were such close friends, he played a huge part in planning the service. The head elders at the church, Pastors Rick and Judy Smith, began to take me under their wing. They organized and planned the logistics of the service and ministered to me. I had one main goal for the funeral: for the gospel of Jesus to be preached and for people to have an opportunity to accept Him as their Savior. Never again would I have the opportunity for Jimmy's friends, coworkers, and family to all be in one place to hear the gospel. I wouldn't let this opportunity pass by.

Next, I had to select a burial plot. This was all extremely difficult for me, and I hurt more with every hour that passed by. During those first few days, I would think at times, *Why am I not crying? I should be drowning in my tears, but I'm not.* The pain was there, but the tears weren't yet. I was still in shock.

The visitation was the following Tuesday evening. Christopher called that morning to tell me that they had Jimmy's body ready and that I could come see him if I wanted to. I most definitely wanted to see him. My parents drove me to the funeral home that morning. My heart pounded because I didn't know how I would handle it. I knew it would be a comfort for me to see him again. I had meticulously chosen what he would be buried in, a suit that I gave him for his birthday while we were engaged that was custom-made just for him.

They respectfully let me go into the room to see him by myself. They had him in the casket and dressed in his suit for the visitation. I looked down at the face that I had comforted for all that time and at the hands that I had held every day. I told him that I was sorry that I couldn't bear the illness for him and that I couldn't stop this from happening. I gave all that I possibly could, and I still couldn't stop it. Tears rolled down my face as our memories together ran through my head. *Would I even be able to go on?*

The time for the visitation came that evening, and I did all I could to help his parents and sister through it. His sister, Kathy, was amazingly strong through it all. She helped to provide strength for the rest of us. I hurt to see Mrs. Geneva and Mr. James hurt. We stood beside Jimmy as our close friends and relatives came one by one. I was numb. Tears wouldn't come. I just stood there and thanked others for coming. I figured sooner or later that I would be able to grieve.

The funeral was held the following day. Coworkers, including executives from our company, attended, as well as a lot of friends and family. It meant a lot to me to see everyone there and to receive their comfort. Christopher did a special thing that day for Jimmy. Jimmy's dream car was a BMW M3. Christopher couldn't get that exact model, but he managed to get a beautiful BMW to escort us to the memorial park where Jimmy is buried. I thanked him for his care and generosity.

Just as I did during the funeral, I just sat still at the burial. I don't even know if I had an expression on my face. While I thanked everyone for being there, I couldn't really grieve myself until I was alone. I appreciated everyone's support for me, but I was mostly numb during the ceremonies. I couldn't grip the reality of it all. After the burial, our close family and friends gathered at our house to eat a meal that our church provided.

After everyone left that day, I had some time to myself, and I was able to let it all begin to sink in. I went back to the gravesite and saw that the tent was still up. The flowers were on the ground spread across the fresh dirt on top of where Jimmy was buried. As I watched the sun set in the distance, I stood quietly as tears streamed down my cheeks. I wanted Jimmy by my side, but he was so far away. Just days earlier, I could hug him. I couldn't hug him now. I couldn't feel him near me. One day he was with me, and in the blink of an eye he was taken away, ripped out of my reach. How could I live another day like this? As the shock wore off, the pain became increasingly unbearable.

As each day passed by, I became more aware that this wasn't a nightmare that I would wake up from. I went to bed at night asking God to take me during the night. I was angry with Him when I woke up the following morning. My desire to live another day on this earth became less and less. If there was going to be a car accident, I asked God to let it be me who didn't survive. I couldn't live in the pain, and I would have done anything to hold Jimmy in my arms again.

I spent two weeks at home before going back to work. Many people had no idea what to say to me. However, I knew everyone had the deepest compassion for me. They did all they could to comfort me as best as they knew how. One of the managers in my office probably said it best. He came by my desk, stood there for a moment, and then said, "I just don't know what to say." Then he went back to his office. I knew he cared, and without saying something thoughtless to hurt me further, he politely and honestly said all he could think of. I appreciated that.

The two vice presidents that I worked for, Wayne Scott and Martin Powell, became a huge blessing. They were understanding when I had a hard time at work. God gave me grace beyond what I could ask for. In moments when I should have fallen apart, I didn't.

Cleaning out Jimmy's office at work was painful but necessary. Because we worked in the same office, walking into his department should have crushed me, but it didn't. When I couldn't even ask Jesus, He surrounded me with a protective barrier to shield me from the hurt. Even though I felt angry with Him day after day, there was "only one set of footprints" in the sand, and they weren't mine.[6] This became my living testimony to those around me. Others would ask, "How do you stay so strong?" I told them, "It's not my strength that's sustaining me." Our Executive Vice President, Martin Powell, said, "It's like you're a rock." I told him, "I'm standing on a Rock—Jesus." I couldn't let my continuing hurt and anger toward God keep me from sharing the gospel.

My daily comfort was visiting the gravesite and making sure it looked clean and tidy. I didn't want a flower to be out of place. That was all I had left to take care of for him. Every day, I made my daily stop by the memorial park with a wet cloth to clean the marker. I soon learned that a toothbrush worked well to get mud out from corners. Having Jimmy's resting place looking almost perfect was the only way I could still take care of him. Some days I would just stand for a few minutes and let out what emotions I could put words to. I would ask God to give him messages for me and at the same time beg Him to take me. I looked up into the sky and wondered where heaven was and what Jimmy was experiencing. I told Jimmy that I was sorry that it happened this way and that I was sorry I couldn't stop it. I had no control over what happened and what was happening now. I felt forced into this daily cycle of hating where I was and having no ability to change it.

Going home to an empty house after work each day only compounded the throbbing inside my chest. Some days I would

---

6. See note 2.

sit at the bottom of my stairs in disbelief and stare at the front door, just knowing that Jimmy would walk in any minute. I couldn't believe that Jimmy wasn't coming back.

About a week after going back to work, the shock slowly continued to wear off. That was when I started feeling the unbearable pain. It would grip me to the point that I almost couldn't breathe. It suffocated me. All I could do was curl up in a ball on the floor and let out the cries that had been trapped inside of me. I wailed. I could only truly grieve when I was by myself, and it would all pour out of me like a flood. The pain wasn't just emotional—I felt it shoot through my physical body as well. Every day I felt as if someone had dragged me into a dark alley and beaten me until I was nearly dead. That is how I felt day after day—beaten and bruised. Not much life was left inside me.

One day after work when I was making my daily stop by Jimmy's gravesite, I felt as if I couldn't live another minute in such agony. The hurt was overtaking me, and I couldn't see life beyond the pain. As I stood by Jimmy's marker, my quiet tears turned into sobbing. I knelt down and touched his marker as if to seek something tangible of Jimmy that I could touch. A cool rain began to fall, but that didn't faze me. In that moment, I didn't want to live another minute. Before that time, I never understood why someone would want to take their own life. But now I understand that feeling of unending despair. In that moment, I began to plan. I still had all of Jimmy's medications, and I began to plan which ones I would take first, second, and third. I had no reason to live another minute. That is what I thought, anyway.

178 *The Call of a Caregiver*

As I drove home, my mind was made up. I was going to end my suffering that night. However, as I walked into my bedroom, something that I couldn't see with my own eyes stopped me. Something intangible held me back almost physically from reaching for those pills. This is proof of the power of God's love for us. In my deepest despair, I felt the love of God breathing the desire to live back inside of me. I couldn't explain it. Even though I was fighting back, Jesus was not letting me go.

One day while I was getting my laundry together, I opened the laundry basket where we kept our white laundry. God had an unexpected surprise for me that provided further comfort that I needed. I looked down to see a shirt of Jimmy's that my mom had missed while doing our laundry. I now had something of Jimmy's that he had worn that gave me something to hold on to.

Over the following month, I continually ran into challenges. Jimmy had handled all of our finances, and now I had to sort through bills and debt that needed to be paid and handle things like our insurance and taxes. To say I was overwhelmed would be an understatement. However, as I sorted through our files to see where to start, I was amazed at how up-to-date and organized all of the paperwork was. It was as if Jimmy had prepared ahead of time for me to take things over. This became one of the ways that God showed me He was caring for me all along.

Another challenge was yard work. That was another responsibility that Jimmy had taken care of. I had never cut the grass before, and having to learn how to use a lawn mower was another huge reminder that I was by myself without Jimmy's help. My mom helped me cut the grass the first time, but I eventually had to learn to do it on my own. I would try to cut it after work each week, letting tears run down my cheeks with each step that I took. It hurt my heart more than anything else. Even with that challenge, God always sent me help. Some days I would come home from work, and my next door neighbor, Jason, had already cut my front yard for me. Also, each week, my cousin Kevin, who lived thirty minutes away, would come and do my yard work and repairs around the house. God never expected me to do this alone. He will always take care of your needs, and whatever you are going through, you never have to face it by yourself.

God sent people to help me through phone calls, cards, and visits. Reverend Jerry Temple, the pastor of the church where I grew up, made a special visit, and I welcomed his encouragement. Cards and phone calls poured in. Everyone's care and support helped me through my days.

During these first several weeks after Jimmy went to heaven, I couldn't even pray. My attitude was, "Why pray? God is going to do what He wants to anyway." That is not how God operates. He longs for us to have a relationship with Him full of prayer and communication with Him. But I questioned God daily. I was angry with Him and hurt at the same time. I missed my daily walk with Him, but I felt as if He had betrayed me. My hurt brought me to a vulnerable place, a place where Satan could easily put thoughts into my mind against God. I wondered some days if I even wanted to still be a Christian. What was the point? I couldn't even bring myself to read my Bible. I would just sit and look at it thinking, *Are the promises in there even true? It doesn't look like it to me.* I didn't understand the spiritual warfare that was taking place over my soul during that time. Satan almost won. He didn't succeed in my plans to take my own life, and he was now tempting me to renounce my faith in Christ.

I hurt twenty-four hours a day with no letup. My dreams of Jimmy at night would give me a little comfort until I woke up to my never-ending nightmare. From when I woke up to when I went to sleep, I was internally and almost physically tortured from the grief. Some nights I would sit by my bed and weep uncontrollably. I just wanted Jimmy back or to go to heaven and be where he was. Why wouldn't God take me?

I began to notice that as I wept, I felt something like a blanket wrap around me. It was like a blanket of comfort and love taking the harshest blows of my pain. I knew that the Holy Spirit was there. Even when I hurt too badly to ask Him for help, He surrounded me with love that can only come from our Heavenly Father. "But You, O Lord, are a God full of compassion, and gracious, longsuffering and abundant in mercy and truth" (Psalm 86:15). In my emptiness, I began to welcome His presence. It was like water to a parched tongue. I started to see that He was my only help out of this pit of despair. Only He could comfort me in the inner-most depths of my heart. Was I going to accept His help? I lifted my eyes toward heaven and began to open my empty heart to the One Who loved me more than I could understand.

CHAPTER 17

God's Eternal Purposes

(AUGUST–NOVEMBER 2006)

ONE OF THE MOST DIFFICULT aspects of losing a spouse at such an early age is that I not only grieved for Jimmy, but I grieved for my entire future, my hopes and dreams. Since I was a child I knew I wanted to be a mom. After Jimmy went to heaven, I figured I would never have children, and that caused additional pain for me. I couldn't imagine ever marrying again. Jimmy was the love of my life. I figured that if Jesus wasn't going to take me to heaven, then I would live the rest of my life alone. I couldn't see my future past the end of my nose. When I thought about what was ahead for me, I saw only darkness.

Each time I cried out in pain, I would just plainly tell God how I felt. That was how I started opening up to Him. I had to be honest with God. I told Him I was angry with Him and felt betrayed by Him. When I would have these times with God, He gave me a vision of a loving father holding a child during a temper tantrum. There I was, like a child, having a fit in the arms of my Father, yet He wouldn't abandon me. He is longsuffering, and He knows better than we do about what we go through. He kept holding me, giving me time to calm down just like a loving parent would.

Tammy Trent, in her book *Learning to Breathe Again*, describes this best. "God remains forever constant. That's the one thing that's kept me going, and it's the most important thing I share with audiences around the country. No matter what, God's still here, and at the end of the day, God is enough. Always has been, always will be. He can handle whatever we dish out. He laughs with us in the good times, he carries us through the pain, and when tragedy knocks the wind out of us, he helps us learn to breathe again."[7] She, too, had lost her husband at a young age. God used her story to minister to me immensely.

Just because I finally started opening back up to Jesus didn't mean that my pain went away. Many times when I closed my eyes, I could still hear the alarms from the ICU going off. I still felt the emptiness and agony day after day.

I had to continue my job in a professional manner, trying my best not to break down too much at work. One day in particular about two months after Jimmy passed away, our company had a meeting for our managers. I tried to put a smile on my face to cover up my sadness. On that day, I especially felt like giving up on everything. If it were possible, I wanted to just give up on life.

One of our managers in our Canadian office, Elaine, always had a caring and friendly personality. During that meeting, out of nowhere she handed me a little card with a note on it. It said, "Allow yourself to heal." She didn't know just how low I felt that day, and I truly believe God used her and that little note to help lift me back up. I posted it on my refrigerator, and every time I wanted to throw in the towel and not make it to the next day, I

---

7 Tammy Trent, *Learning to Breathe Again: Choosing Life and Finding Hope After a Shattering Loss* (Nashville: Thomas Nelson, 2004), 211.

would read it. It reminded me that even though I hurt that badly at that point in time, *don't give up*. It takes time to go through the grieving process, and I needed to allow that process to run its course. I had to believe if I were to allow the time to pass and keep putting one foot in front of the other, there would be something for me beyond the grief. I'm glad I did.

One special person whom God brought into my life during that time was my friend April. I met her through a grief support group, and she too had recently lost her husband. We were close to the same age and had the same hopes of having a family. The emotions that we dealt with were similar, and we spent a lot of time on the phone and visiting each other. To become friends with someone who knew my pain was a tremendous help to me and I believe it was to her as well. To this day we're still very close friends.

Reading my Bible was another step for me to take in my faith. I went from looking at my Bible to setting it in my lap. I missed my close relationship with God, but I didn't even know who I thought He was anymore. Did I really know who He was? I sat in my living room with my Bible in my lap, and tears began to run down my face. My prayer was this: "Lord, please don't let my misunderstanding come between You and me." I know somewhere during all of this, I had misunderstood something about Him. I wasn't mad at Him because He had changed Who He was. God is the same yesterday, today, and forevermore. Something about my knowledge of God wasn't right. After I prayed this prayer, He gradually started showing me more of how magnificent He really is. Going through this tragedy brought me to an entirely new understanding of God's heart.

You see, I had planned and knew what I wanted out of life and expected God would make it happen. No one says, "Well, I guess I'll go through having my entire life ripped out from under me. Then I'll plan to stick it out and see what comes next." No, my plans were to get married, have children, and live happily ever after. Now all of that had been taken away from me with no desire to have it with anyone but Jimmy. I resisted the thought of having any plans in my future without Jimmy. One night when I was struggling particularly with this, I heard the Holy Spirit speak to me. He said, "Just give Me a chance, and you'll see that you do want what I have for you." Even though I couldn't imagine wanting anything while still on this earth, God asked me to just give Him a chance to bring the things into my life that He desired. And even though I didn't think I wanted it then, I would when the time came. I had to allow God to work in my life through faith. I knew I had to say yes.

I needed to organize our paperwork that had accumulated over time in Jimmy's office at home. Not only did we have papers from our personal finances, but I now had hospital records and bills everywhere. As I sorted through them, I started feeling the crushing weight of grief on my shoulders. I felt as if someone had put a thousand pounds on my back, and I found it difficult to even breathe. It was unbearable. In that moment, I heard the Lord speak to me. He said, "You're trying to carry this burden by yourself, and you can't do it by yourself. I have called you to this life. Let Me carry the burden of your pain." Isaiah 53:4a says,

"Surely He has borne our griefs and carried our sorrows." He didn't bring me to that point in time to just leave me to handle it all on my own. I needed to allow Him to carry my sorrows for me. He never intended for me to carry it alone.

I began to understand more about Jesus' prayer in the Garden of Gethsemane. In Matthew 26:39, Jesus prayed, "'O My Father, if it is possible, let this cup pass from Me; nevertheless, not as I will, but as You will.'" He was about to face the greatest suffering beyond our comprehension, yet He submitted to it according to the will of His Father. I began to understand that I should be willing to pray like Jesus prayed. No matter the cost, would I submit to this unexpected plan for my life? Jesus laid down His life and went through the greatest suffering of all for the greatest purpose of all—salvation of mankind. Who was I that I wouldn't lay down my life and go through my suffering for the purposes that God had planned out for my life? I knew in my spirit that God was working something bigger than I could understand, and it would reach far beyond this earthly life. There were eternal purposes that I couldn't ignore. If through my submitting to God's will, no matter how painful, there would be another person standing next to me in heaven, it would be worth it all.

When I had times that I regretted still being alive, God showed me something. He showed me that if He still had me alive here on the earth, there must be a purpose. He hadn't taken me to heaven yet because my assignment here wasn't complete. That gave me motivation to keep from giving up. If you are still here on this earth, there is a purpose and a plan that only you can fulfill. Don't let Satan talk you out of that. Cling to your faith, and you will, in God's timing, see the purposes that He has for you.

Through my process of grief and the beginnings of my healing, God began to come through in my life as only He can. Many times the ways that He works make no sense to us. I finally had to be okay with not having the answers. Even after the autopsy results were completed, the doctors still didn't have a diagnosis for Jimmy. His multi-organ failure was caused by an infection that antibiotics couldn't fight, and that was all the doctors could tell me. I still didn't have a diagnosis for his initial liver failure and compromised immune system. I didn't know why Jimmy got sick or why he wasn't healed. And if God wanted me to know it, He would tell me. By faith, I have to be okay with unanswered questions. I have to leave that in God's hands.

In Dr. James Dobson's book *When God Doesn't Make Sense*, he titled one of his chapters "God Makes Sense Even When He Doesn't Make Sense."[8] In the book of Genesis, Joseph's life wasn't making much sense when he was thrown into a pit, sold into slavery, and then unjustly put into prison. But God used all of that to make him ruler over Egypt and to save people in time of famine. We can't see the whole picture. The little part of life that we're in today may not make sense, but the bigger picture does. That is why "we walk by faith, not by sight" (2 Corinthians 5:7).

One truth that has given me the most peace of all is that I know where Jimmy is. Through his suffering in the hospital, he continued to draw closer to Jesus. He was more ready to be

8. James Dobson, *When God Doesn't Make Sense* (Wheaton, IL: Tyndale House, 1993), 43.

ushered into heaven than anyone else I've known. I know I'll
see him again one day. And that's because of the One Who truly
gave it all, Jesus.

Because Jesus paid the price for our sins, mine and Jimmy's
separation is only temporary. Jesus died on the cross and was
raised from the dead for us to have peace in this life as well as
eternal life with God. If you're going through what seems like
an impossible situation and you're going through it alone, you
don't have to. Life, no matter how hard it gets, never has to be
void of hope and purpose. If you would like to reach out to Jesus
and accept His gift of eternal life, ask Him to forgive you of your
sins and to be your Lord and Savior. He longs for a relationship
with you and to be your source of life and strength.

I still consider myself to be Jimmy's caregiver. I'm caring
for his story and his testimony. I'm glad I didn't give up and
that through the Lord's help I'm fulfilling the call as Jimmy's
caregiver. I have continually seen how God has used our story
to help those around us, and I praise Him for that. I'm thankful that I didn't throw in the towel because I would have never
experienced what God had for me next.

PJ and Jessica's Wedding Picture
January 29, 2008

CHAPTER 18

My Boaz

(DECEMBER 2006–DECEMBER 2010)

OFTENTIMES WHILE SEARCHING IN GOD'S Word for comfort, I found myself in the book of Ruth. I could relate to her because she too became a widow at a young age. I'm sure she had hopes and dreams for her future with her husband, and I can imagine that she had some of the same feelings I did. I saw that she was a young woman whom God had a purpose for who also experienced my same devastation.

Ruth is known for her faithfulness to her mother-in-law, Naomi. After the death of Naomi's husband and two sons (one being Ruth's husband), Naomi is returning to the land of Judah. Ruth said to her, "'Entreat me not to leave you, or to turn back from following after you; for wherever you go, I will go; and wherever you lodge, I will lodge; your people shall be my people, and your God, my God. Where you die, I will die, and there will I be buried. The Lord do so to me, and more also, if anything but death parts you and me'" (Ruth 1:16–17). I myself have a strong devotion to Jimmy's family. His mom and I have always been especially close, many times talking daily after Jimmy went to heaven. I care deeply for her and his dad, Mr. James. Also, his sister, Kathy, encouraged me with her wisdom and comfort. They will always be my family, and we continue to enjoy our close relationship today.

Ruth was committed not only to her mother-in-law, but she committed herself to the will of God. She traveled to the land of Judah by faith, not knowing what her future held. Many days passed for me that I was only stepping out in faith. I kept pressing into a closer relationship with Jesus, knowing that someday my purpose for staying faithful would become evident. If I were to continue to live more days on this earth, I would make them count, somehow. I would have to seek what God wanted to do with my life now.

Ruth's faithfulness eventually led her to a life full of abundance. She picked up leftover grain in a field that belonged to a man named Boaz. After catching his eye and finding favor with him, he married her. He cared and provided for her, and they had a son named Obed. Ruth became part of the lineage of Jesus.

Many of my days felt dark and lonely, but as I continued through my daily walk of seeking God's wisdom for my life, little by little things began to unfold. Several months after Jimmy passed away, while I was at work, a coworker that I hadn't seen in a while came to speak with me. His name was PJ (for Paul Joseph), and he had known Jimmy. He took a few minutes to express his sympathy toward me, and I appreciated his taking the time for that. He had also been through some difficult times, and we spoke about holding on to faith in Christ when times are tough. Off and on as our paths crossed at work, we would take a minute or two to chat or encourage one another.

One Sunday in December 2006, PJ told me that the daughter of Payne Stewart, a professional golfer who died in an airplane accident, was sharing her testimony at his church, NewSpring Church in Anderson, South Carolina. He asked me if I wanted to go to the service, and I decided that since we were becoming friends I would go. I really enjoyed the service and hearing her testimony. That night began a whirlwind of emotions for me.

When I was busy at home or at work, I started thinking about how much I enjoyed PJ's company. I didn't like that at all. I couldn't think about another man like that. I was devoted to Jimmy and had decided that I would never have a relationship with another man. The more I thought about PJ, the more aggravated I got. I prayed for those thoughts to go away. *What?* I thought. *This cannot be.* I wanted to turn those feelings off and go my own way. But the more I prayed about it, the stronger my feelings became, and I didn't know how to handle it.

Finally, I decided to stop resisting it. Okay, so I enjoyed being around PJ. We talked a lot about our faith in Christ during hard times, and we found ourselves laughing about the same things and felt encouraged by one another. He wanted to support me as a brother in Christ and a friend, comforting me in my grief. And I wanted to be a friend to him as well. Was God maybe up to something here?

After a few months, I felt we needed to be open and honest about how we felt about one another and about how our relationship might evolve in the future. I was a grieving widow, and my heart was very vulnerable. It was imperative that a relationship between us only happen according to God's will.

Without His blessing, we would only set ourselves up for disappointment and hurt.

After talking, we revealed that we had both developed more romantic feelings toward one another. Neither one of us was interested in a casual dating relationship. We didn't want to date unless we both believed this could possibly lead to marriage. We decided that before dating, we would spend time separately seeking God to learn what His will was for us. And that's what we did.

Spending that time separately seeking God gave us the answers we needed. Proverbs 3:5–6 says, "Trust in the Lord with all your heart, and lean not on your own understanding; in all your ways acknowledge Him, and He shall direct your paths." That is a promise. Not only did we find it hard being away from

PJ and Jessica Skiing in
Jackson Hole, WY

one another, our prayers and our time spent apart only confirmed the desires of our hearts. We believed that God may very well have planned for us to be together.

Over the time we dated, our belief that God wanted us to be married was confirmed. On December 31, 2007, PJ proposed to me. We were married less than a month later on January 29, 2008.

I knew all along that for PJ to be called by God to be my husband, he would have to be a special man. And he is. Not just any man could step into the role that PJ did. I was still grieving for Jimmy while we dated, and he understood that I intended to continue to share my story, not just leave it behind. All that I had been through molded my character into who I am today, and PJ embraces that. Not only has he helped me take care of Jimmy's gravesite, but he has shown kindness and care toward Jimmy's family. Above all, he's supportive of my call to share Jimmy's story and all that we endured. The call on PJ's life and the grace provided to him is nothing to be taken lightly. God knew what I needed and what was needed for His ministry and His greater plan, and He saw PJ, my Boaz.

When Boaz met Ruth, he highly respected the family she came from and the fact that she was a widow. He desired to be responsible for her. The way that PJ came into my life reminded me of how Boaz sought to care for and provide for Ruth. And together, they came into the purposes that God had for them. God saw where both PJ and I came from, how we desired to be obedient to Him, and what the possibilities were for our lives.

The journey has been amazing. PJ has nurtured me and helped to heal my wounds and build my faith. I'm continually thankful that God chose such a strong, godly, and kindhearted man to walk along beside me,

PJ and Jessica Scuba Diving in Vietnam

and every day I seek to be the best wife to him that I can possibly be. I am honored that God chose me to be his wife and only hope that I can bless his life as much as he has blessed mine.

God has given us more than we could have imagined or asked for. On May 14, 2009, we became parents to our beautiful little girl, Catherine, and we are now expecting another little girl in March 2011. I'm a stay-at-home mom, a desire of my heart since I was a child. In June 2006, I thought my life was over. Today I stand amazed at what God has done. And only He could have brought these things to pass.

I continue to seek ways to share my story in hopes that others can find comfort and healing in their own difficult situations. I want others to know that they are not alone in their suffering. Jesus is our Sustainer. The Bible doesn't say that because we are

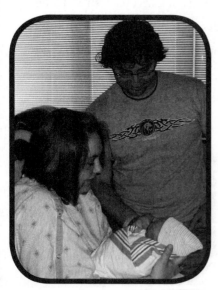

The day our little Catherine was born
May 14, 2009

Christians we won't suffer. In fact, the Bible clearly says that we will experience suffering while on this earth. Sometimes God does an instant miracle, and that's wonderful. But many times He provides us grace through the process. Sometimes the most profound miracle is being sustained *in the midst of* the pain.

The more you completely abandon all for the Lord, the more you will come to the true rest that He has for you. As long as you try to handle things your own way, the more of a struggle life will be. I finally realized that my trials weren't about me. It's not about how I feel or what I have. It's about Jesus and eternity. Paul said in Philippians 1:12, "But I want you to know, brethren, that the things which happened to me have actually turned out for the furtherance of the gospel." Once I turned my focus away from myself and understood that this was about the furtherance of the gospel, I found freedom and rest. I struggled for months before I finally handed it all to God: my hurts, frustrations, plans, and whole future.

James 5:10–11 says, "My brethren, take the prophets, who spoke in the name of the Lord, as an example of suffering and patience. *Indeed we count them blessed who endure.* You have heard of the perseverance of Job and seen the end intended by the Lord—that the Lord is very com-passionate and merciful" (italics mine). In spite of how things ap-pear, God is always working out what is best for you and for His plan. If you're enduring a hard-ship, you're considered blessed. It is not for nothing.

My story isn't finished yet. God has amazed PJ and me with all that He is doing through us and for us. However, our time here on earth is not completed, and I know that as long as we

Jessica, PJ and Catherine
December 2010

live on earth we will have difficulties. No one is exempt from hardships. However, we have a way to make it through the hardships—Jesus.

I will continue to keep my eyes turned toward heaven, toward the One Who has sustained, healed, and blessed me more than I could have ever asked. Not a day goes by that I don't praise Him for saving me from my deepest despair and for bringing me to the life that I'm living today.

Understand that there is always purpose to your hardships in Christ. Look to Jesus through the good times and the bad. He's forever faithful, and He will never leave you behind. Hold His hand and allow Him to lead you to a place of comfort, hope, purpose, and rest.

"Though the fig tree may not blossom, nor fruit be on the vines; though the labor of the olive may fail, and the fields yield no food; though the flock may be cut off from the fold, and there be no herd in the stalls—yet I will rejoice in the Lord, I will joy in the God of my salvation. The Lord God is my strength; He will make my feet like deer's feet, and He will make me walk on my high hills" (Habakkuk 3:17–19).

Epilogue by PJ Mast

I WAS IN A HOTEL room in Ireland when I read an email announcing to the company that Jimmy had passed away. I couldn't believe what I was reading. I mean, I didn't even know he was that sick! I didn't know Jimmy very well and I knew Jessica even less, but at that moment, my heart broke for her. I just couldn't imagine what she was going through and I wanted to help her if I could. I prayed for Jessica a lot through the rest of that trip and the weeks ahead.

When Jessica came back to work I wanted to talk to her but didn't know what to say, so I put it off. We were on opposite sides of the building and our paths almost never crossed. Finally, after a few months, I went and talked to her. Pretty much all I knew about her was that she was married to Jimmy and that she was a Christian. I wanted to reach out to her as a brother in Christ but had no idea what to say. I don't remember all the circumstances leading up to it but I do remember finally standing at her desk talking to her. I briefly explained how God was helping me through a difficult time and I knew He would do the same for her. We must have talked for ten or fifteen minutes and when I walked away I felt really good knowing that I had done just a little bit to help her that day.

We talked occasionally after that and I offered to help her in any way I could. She had lost the key to Jimmy's motorcycle and didn't know what to do so I told her that I would take care of it. When I picked it up from her house it seemed like she really needed to talk so I asked if she wanted to go get something to eat. In the months that followed, I helped her with a few things and we shared a few meals together. Our conversation was always serious and focused largely on what she had been through and how God was working in each of our lives. One day we were at a steakhouse, and after sitting there reading the menu for a few minutes she calmly said, "I'm going to have the twenty-eight-ounce aged prime rib." I looked at her and burst out laughing! She tried to keep a straight face and asked why I was laughing before she finally erupted in laughter too. That was the first time I remember us laughing together and, honestly, I don't think we have stopped laughing since that day. That was a turning point in our friendship.

What I learned about Jessica during this time was that, on her own, she wasn't a particularly strong person. She had that appearance, but those who know her best know that she is a delicate little flower pedal. The strength that she portrayed was extraordinary and it had to be coming from God. This is a clear example of God using an ordinary person who is committed to Him to do extraordinary things.

There is no doubt in my mind that if God had healed Jimmy, he and Jessica would have given God all the credit and He would have been glorified through that situation. But isn't it easy to give God the glory when things go right? Isn't it easy to praise

God and thank Him when He does exactly what we want Him to do? The real story that came out of all this was that even when God doesn't do what we want Him to, He's still God and He's still good! Jeremiah 29:11 says, "'For I know the plans I have for you," declares the Lord, "plans to prosper you and not to harm you, plans to give you hope and a future'" (NIV). Jessica felt like this event would destroy her, but once she decided to follow God no matter what, she soon began to see how His plan would ultimately be for her good. She thanked God for what He was going to do in her life even though she had no idea what that would be. She began to praise God even when she didn't feel like it, and in doing so she was surrendering her life to Him. Jessica learned to worship God and draw near to Him just because of Who He is. Not to get something from Him or out of obligation, but just because He is God.

In the years since Jimmy's passing, Jessica has grown and matured into an amazing woman of God. She was the leader of the hospital team for our church and still volunteers with that group. Even though it was difficult for her to go back into a hospital, she sacrificed her own comfort in order to be a comfort to those who could benefit from what she had been through. I have met several people that she ministered to and they were all amazed by the grace and peace that accompanies her into a hospital room. Jessica is determined to not let her pain go to waste; she is going to use that pain to help everyone she possibly can.

Watching her write this book over the past year and a half has shown me just how important it is to her to get her and Jimmy's story out. It has been a sacrifice of her time as she worked around the full-time schedule of raising our first child as well as making our house a home. She has had to relive many painful memories, and the emotional strain alone was enough for me to question this work at times. What amazes me is that she did all this to help people whom she doesn't even know. Jessica is a blessing to everyone around her, and her life challenges even the most godly to pursue a deeper relationship with their Creator. God would have been glorified if Jimmy had lived, but God is still being glorified, and to a much greater degree, through his death.

For more information about
Jessica Mast
&

The Call of a Caregiver
please visit:

www.JessicaMMast.com
jmastbooks@gmail.com
@JessicaMMast
www.facebook.com/jmastbooks

For more information about
AMBASSADOR INTERNATIONAL
please visit:

www.ambassador-international.com
@AmbassadorIntl
www.facebook.com/AmbassadorIntl